BLADESMITHING
with Murray Carter

Modern Application of Traditional Techniques

Published by

Krause Publications, a division of F+W Media, Inc.
700 East State Street • Iola, WI 54990-0001
715-445-2214 • 888-457-2873
www.krausebooks.com

To order books or other products call toll-free 1-800-258-0929
or visit us online at www.krausebooks.com or www.Shop.Collect.com

Cover & Interior photography by
Hiro Soga & Murray Carter

ISBN-13: 978-1-4402-1838-5
ISBN-10: 1-4402-1838-2

Cover & Interior Design by Tom Nelsen
Edited by Corrina Peterson

Printed in the United States of America

Dedication

This book is dedicated to all the people who have positively shaped my life. Surely each one mentioned here knows in what way, shape or form they influenced me, without specifically mentioning it here. Thanks go out to Major Skipper, David Dibblee, Suzette Dibblee, Charles Bunce, Danny Mosher, Tim Curnew, Dave Griffin, Mike Delaney, Billy Doan, Eddy Maskinie, James Hickling, Jim Aamon, Arnold Schwarzenegger, Kyohei Kugishima, Yasuyuki Sakemoto, Seiichi Hayashi, Red Fox Nakashima, Hiroshi Mori, Chitose Sensei, Chimata Uchida, Baikuya Saruwatari, Tim McCalla and Wes Injerd; Corrina Peterson, my editor; my parents and siblings; Bill Gibson and the mighty men of HOFCC; my dear children, Tetsuo, Emily, Alisa and Maria; my gracious wife Rumiko; and especially my Lord and Savior, Jesus Christ.

10/13/16

Dear Dong,
Thanks for showing me your Man Cave! Here's to our next few days of knife-smithing!
Stay Sharp,
Murray
SFO

Contents

Preface

Artist /Craftsman/Artisan

In my opinion, there is a very important distinction between the artist, the craftsman and the artisan.

The Artist

An artist is someone who has an idea or image in their head, and to them it becomes an obsession to transfer that which is in their mind out into the world. Like a baby which has been conceived, the mother must deliver that baby into the world or suffer major physiological and emotional complications. To the artist it often feels like a matter of life and death. They feel like they might explode if they can't adequately express what is inside of them. Time, money, relationships, even their own health often takes second place to their artwork. Due to the nature of the artist's priorities, it is often necessary for an artist to have a financially supportive patron or partner of some kind. The concept of daily wages has little meaning to the bona fide artist. While they are sometimes eccentric and difficult to understand, societies around the world owe a tremendous debt to artists. They have expanded our understanding of the world around us in every single subject, as they have innovated, invented and expanded the boundaries of what we knew as reality.

The Craftsman

The craftsman is someone who takes great delight in making things with their hands for people to use. They might be furniture makers, house builders or toy makers. They take pride in their work and seek recognition from colleagues and superiors, and usually improvement in their skills comes with time. One of the rewards for the craftsman is being able to see tangible results from his efforts. A craftsman is a practical person and is very much aware of the delicate balance of time and money. At the end of each day he counts his wages and starts to plan how he will spend his money on things that will give him even more pleasure than his work. The world owes much appreciation to the craftsmen of the world who provide us with an abundance of finely crafted household items.

The Artisan

The artisan is a rare mix between the artist and the craftsman. At first glance the work of an artisan may seem to qualify him as an artist because of uniqueness and outstanding workmanship. However, the all-telling clue as to the artisan's true identity is that his children are not starving and his bills are paid. The artisan, while he may have an artistic bent which he indulges from time to time, is also acutely aware of costs, expenses and earnings. The difference is that when the artisan expresses his artistic side, he can afford to, as he has budgeted his time for it.

I consider myself an artisan. If your aspiration is to get into full time bladesmithing, it is vitally important to identify which one of the above three workers you are. Disappointment and financial duress may result if you are unrealistic in your assessment of your personality. When in doubt, ask several people around you who know you best which one they think you are.

Murray Carter
April 2011

Introduction

This book is written to provide the reader with an in-depth look into the why's and how's of traditional Japanese cutlery forging techniques and their modern applications. Because of the non-stop flow of inquiries I've received to share the secret techniques I learned during 18 years in Japan, where I lived and worked as a village bladesmith, it seemed appropriate to share that wealth of information for the benefit of the curious reader and Japanese knife enthusiast alike. It is my hope that those who own the nearly 15,000 knives I've made will be delighted to see a comprehensive book written by their creator.

I've attempted to write in a manner that will appeal to an international knife audience, to collectors and users of fine Japanese woodworking tools, and to some degree, those who are fascinated with the small handful of foreigners who have made unique inroads into the traditional Japanese arts, which have seemed impenetrable ever since the American Commodore Matthew C. Perry forced Japan to open its doors to the rest of the world in 1854.

I hope to provide a unique and extremely rare insight into the Japanese culture through the (blue) eyes of a Japanese village bladesmith, including detailed explanations of traditional bladesmithing techniques that until now have been cloaked in mystery and myths. My goal is provide enough detailed information to guide a new aspiring bladesmith to become successful in the Japanese style of blade making.

A 17th-generation Yoshimoto bladesmith, I am the only Caucasian ever to have been recognized as a Japanese bladesmithing master. I speak and read the Japanese language fluently, and have been gifted in the area of communicating with the native Japanese to a degree that is extremely uncommon in any industry. I am equally adept at forging traditional Japanese cutlery and outdoor knives. I am also the sole instructor of Murray Carter's Bladesmithing School in Oregon, where I convey ancient Japanese bladesmithing skills and techniques.

Early Years

Born in Halifax, Nova Scotia, Canada, if one were to look at my comprehensive genealogy, he or she would recognize in my ancestors a repeating combination of hands-on craftsmen (farmers, a cobbler), a strong value placed on higher education, solid fiscal sense and strong religious convictions on both sides of the family. One look at my lifestyle and business practices today reveals that I remain true to my lineage, being a master craftsman, an accomplished teacher and businessman, and a Born Again believer in Jesus Christ.

As the only boy and the youngest, I often escaped into my own world, which consisted of TV, comic books and playing Lego. My favorite TV shows shared the common themes of survival, war, superhero-ism or adventure. Most memorable was the TV series "Battle for Midway." Another favorite was the "Bionic Man." Naturally, with this kind of background, I became fully drawn in, to the point of obsession, with the "Star Wars" series. I thought, "If only I, too, could travel to a galaxy far, far away!" Little did I know how those feelings would eventually take me a world away from my hometown of Halifax, all the way to Kumamoto, Japan.

Me at age seven.

I remember the comic books Sgt. Rock, GI Combat, Unknown Soldier, Spiderman, Capt. America, Western Kid, and Turok, Son of Stone (tales about two native Indians lost in a hidden valley killing dinosaurs!). At eight years old, I recall fashioning a simple bow and arrows from wood and fantasizing about shooting dinosaurs from my tree house. I loved throwing a small hatchet that I had found in the family's summer vacation cottage woodshed. Looking back, it is a wonder nobody was ever hurt by such behavior.

In 1982, a transformational event took place when I went to see the movie "Conan the Barbarian," starring Arnold Schwarzenegger. I related to this hero and was especially fascinated with the sword-forging sequence at the beginning of the film. I particularly remember this line from the movie where Conan's father explains the "riddle of steel" to young Conan.

Conan's father:

Fire and wind come from the sky, from the gods of the sky. But Crom is your god, Crom and he lives in the earth.

Once, giants lived in the Earth, Conan. And in the dark-ness of chaos, they fooled Crom, and they took from him the enigma of steel. Crom was angered. And the Earth shook. Fire and wind struck down these giants, and they threw their bodies into the waters, but in their rage, the gods forgot the secret of steel and left it on the battlefield. We who found it are just men. Not gods. Not giants. Just men. The secret of steel has always carried with it a mys-tery. You must learn its riddle, Conan. You must learn its discipline. For no one—no one in this world can you trust. Not men, not women, not beasts.

He points to the sword and says:

This you can trust.

The movie's impact on me was tremendous, and was to shape several aspects of my life. From the first moment I saw hot steel formed into a blade on the big screen, I never could shake that powerful imagery from my mind. According to my own father, I had a strong fascination with knives from an early age, and would stand in front of a knife showcase at a store until I was eventually pried away by other family members. And what an impression Schwarzenegger's physique left on me at such a young age. The idea of strengthening one's physical self to better handle life's challenges was an idea that stuck with me.

Airborne!

My parents enrolled me at King's Edgehill School in Windsor, Nova Scotia, starting in eighth grade. KES, as it was commonly referred to, was a traditional boarding school with roots in England and over 200 years of his-tory and tradition. From my point of view, the best thing this school offered was a weekly Tuesday military experi-ence called "Cadets" in Canada. Once a week, rather than donning the regular school uniform, cadets wore green army fatigues, and after just a half-day of regular classes, we studied maps and compass, participated in marching drills, fired small-bore rifles and kept busy doing other military-related activities.

King's Edgehill School, my high school.

As a bonus, rather than return home each year for the summer vacation, I attended various federally sponsored "Summer Cadet Camps." At the age of 13, I attended "Cadet Leader" school; at 14, "Cadet Leader Instructor" school; and at 15 "Banff National Army Cadet Camp." But the pinnacle of the summer cadet program was to come the following year. At 16, through a process of competi-tion and elimination, I was one of only two individuals selected from the province of Nova Scotia to attend the prestigious Canadian Airborne Regiment training pro-gram, to learn how to become a qualified parachutist of the Canadian Armed Forces. This training was the real deal. No special considerations were given for the fact that we were school students. We trained with the regu-lar troops.

At that time, it was rumored that Canadian Airborne was only second to the Israeli Airborne training in terms of difficulty. I was one of 31 cadets who graduated from the program out of the 63 who started. The most exciting parachute jump I made was with full equipment, includ-ing main parachute, reserve parachute, rock-filled back-pack, snowshoes and an FN-FAL rifle during the pitch black of night. In all, I jumped nine times.

Karate

Upon completion of Airborne, I immersed myself into the study of Chitu-Ryu-style Karate, which I had started two years earlier. A friend of mine invited me to go with him to watch a fighting competition where sever-al of Canada's top competitors battled for coveted titles. One man, Dave Griffin, at the time a third-degree black belt (currently ranked higher), won the competition. Mr. Griffin was a very large and strong man, with a barrel chest and "trucker" moustache, but with gentleness and finesse that contradicted his appearance. When I discov-ered his dojo (karate school) was in my neighborhood, I immediately enrolled for evening classes. Thus began my fascination with all things Japanese.

Determined to learn as much as I could, I begged Sensei Griffin to let me participate in both the beginner's and advanced class, which were scheduled back-to-back. I can remember coming home exhausted many karate nights, but the persistence paid off as I rapidly made my way up the ranks, even winning a few competitions. In my free time I read as much as I could about Japan. It was still a time before Japan's influence was to be felt all the way over to the east coast of Atlantic Canada. Trying to learn more about Japan while stuck in Nova Scotia was akin to trying to find snow in the desert. Except for a few outdated books in the regional library, there was noth-ing. This was 1985, way before the days of the Internet and "Google" searches!

Travel, Exposure to Blades and Apprenticeship in Japan

Upon graduation from high school, I chose to work that summer and following spring. I had hatched a plan that included a trip to Japan. Having caught the travel bug on a solo trip to Europe during my senior year of high school, my plan was to travel around the world in one year. During that time, another concept started to take shape in my mind—that of self-sustaining farming. A friend had recommended a book titled *Living the Good Life* by Scott and Helen Nearing. In the book, Helen and Scott outlined their successful self-sufficient farming lifestyle. I thought, "work for yourself, produce what you need, be beholden to nobody. I like it!" However, it would be some time before traveling, the interest in Japan and the farming concept would come together.

Finally, with sufficient money in my pocket, good camping equipment and a plan, I set out on my grand round-the-world adventure in March 1988. My parents drove me to the highway where they let me out and said goodbye to me as I unfurled my hitchhiking sign that said boldly in black type on a large blaze-orange background "Japan or Bust!" So I started my journey by hitching rides from Halifax, Nova Scotia, to Vancouver, Canada, some 6,400 kilometers. Now that, folks, is sheer determination.

After many wonderful and exciting adventures I safely arrived in Japan and immediately enrolled at the Chito-Ryu headquarters in Kumamoto, on the southern island of Kyushu. Chitose Sensei was a wonderfully kind man and had made an exception in letting such a young man come from Canada to study at the head dojo.

On what I think was the second or third day in Kumamoto, I borrowed a scooter from a fellow karate student named Takahiro, and while driving around stumbled upon the bladesmith shop that would change the direction of my life through the eventual apprenticeship with my Sensei, Mr. Yasuyuki Sakemoto, 16th generation Yoshimoto bladesmith. In the display window were some of the coolest knives I had ever seen. I pulled a u-turn and parked in the driveway. Opening the sliding glass door, which had a chime attached to it that rung softly, I ventured into the shop, which was filled with the aroma of a unique combination of burning pine charcoal embers and red-hot metal emanating from the traditional Japanese forge.

My eyes were drawn to the assortment of beautifully crafted, razor-sharp cutlery displayed on the shop walls. There before me were row upon row of traditional blades, edges gleaming, wavy temper lines and layers of lamination highly visible, with beautiful hand-carved handles of native wood. I felt that their sharp shapes and lines of obvious function were begging me to pick them up and put them to use. The traditional blade designs, which have remained largely unchanged for centuries, transported my mind to a more romantic age when life was simpler and straightforward, uncluttered by electronic gadgets and computers, an age when a person was as good as their word, and a time when a great blade could mean the difference between life and death

A kind and gracious gentleman entered from a back door and asked me in heavily accented Japanese if he could assist me. I could have sworn that something clicked between us as we struggled to communicate with each other that first and historic time, for when I indicated that I was interested in seeing more of his shop and learning what secrets lay within, he agreed to let me venture further. That first meeting eventually led to a six-year apprenticeship, a privilege that has never been extended to another.

I spent every available minute each day watching my sensei and trying my hand at forging and grinding. I can remember many a frustrating night, unwilling to give up, grinding and polishing a blade into the wee hours of the morning because I was not satisfied with mediocrity. I can remember the blood from grinding my fingertips, and metal dust in my eyes and nostrils, but still not wanting to stop what I was learning until I got it right.

On the eve of the seventh year, my master approached me while I was hammering away at the forge, covered from head to toe in pine charcoal soot. I was in the fifth day working on a traditional Japanese Samurai sword to present to him as a token of my appreciation and to demonstrate the bladesmithing prowess I had gained over the years. He bent down (as I was in the lowered pit of the Japanese forge), put his right hand on my shoulder, and told me, "You are to be the 17th-generation Yoshimoto Bladesmith." Good thing I wasn't swinging the hammer, or I might have struck one of my fingers! Was this a dream?

I decided to forego my round-the-world adventure in the interest of deepening my understanding of Japan, the language and the people.

My shop in Kumamoto, Japan.

Farming, and a Bride

At the age of 25, I had come to an important decision. I was ready to incorporate the farming aspect into my lifestyle of bladesmithing. I was also ready for marriage. After much searching, I found a house for rent near Tabaruzaka Park, 20 minutes from the heart of downtown Kumamoto. It was in a rural setting, complete with barn and enough land for a vegetable garden. I had just been asked by Master Sakemoto to become the next generation Yoshimoto bladesmith, and with Sakemoto's blessing, this farmhouse was where I planned to set up shop. Serious remodeling and landscaping were soon underway, and I even managed to find a lovely young lady to propose to, as well.

As soon as I was into full blade production in my new shop, I concentrated my efforts on the bladesmithing, eventually producing close to 10,000 blades in this shop, with occasional help from some part-time workers. Over the next 10 years, my bride, Rumiko, and I had four children. Although I studied agriculture at the University of British Columbia, it was Rumiko who proved to have quite a green thumb, and we were able to produce some vegetables in our garden. During the three-month hunting period between November 15 and February 15 each year, we enjoyed fresh game at the dinner table as well. It was during these years in Tabaruzaka that I ventured all over the world to attend knife shows and blade-related symposiums. U.S. customers especially appreciated my work, and a plan surfaced that would involve the long and arduous task of getting visas to live and work in the United States.

My First BLADE Show, and the American Dream

In June 1998, I traveled all the way from Southern Japan to Atlanta, Georgia, to attend my first-ever international cutlery trade show—the BLADE Show. I was full of anxiety and self-doubt. When I had planned to make the knives for the show, I thought, "What happens if my knives get lost in transit?" As I lit the fire in the forge to make the knives, my thoughts were, "What if nobody in the U.S. likes my knives?" As I hammered out the blades, I couldn't help but ponder, "Will my knives be too different for the Western market?" And as I hand sharpened the final edges on my knives, I wondered, "Will I sell any knives at the BLADE Show?" Little did I know that that trip to Atlanta was going to set a new sales record for me and jump-start my business.

Although I was selling enough knives in Japan to make a decent living, it was the high level of interest that my western customers demonstrated, plus the opportunity to pursue the American dream, that made me decide to apply for an immigrant visa to move to the United States.

The visa application process was grueling, requiring document after document, hundreds of hours of writing and filling out applications, and thousands of dollars in fees. In being awarded the visa to immigrate to the United States, I had also inadvertently learned the secret to achieving the American dream—that success is derived from smart planning, hard work, sacrifice and sheer determination.

Vernonia bladesmith shop before renovation, August 2005.

In the fall of 2002, after attending a knife show in southern California, Rumiko and I, along with our son Tetsuo and daughter Emily, boarded a plane in Los Angeles and landed in Portland. Portland is a well-established cutlery center, home to Gerber Legendary Blades, Benchmade Knife Co., Al Mar Knives, Leatherman Tool, William Henry Studio, Lone Wolf Knives, Coast Cutlery, Kershaw and Columbia River Knife & Tool. After a week of driving around the area, we agreed that Portland was where we wanted to move.

When all our criteria for a house and bladesmith shop were entered in the realtor's computer, several properties in the mountain town of Vernonia popped up. The third house I looked at was perfect! It sure needed a lot of love and care, but I could see the potential right away.

The Vernonia home and shop birthed many thousand more blades, the debut of Carter Cutlery Traditional Japanese Bladesmithing classes, the growth in Carter Cutlery staff members, the beginning of the Inner Circle Membership program and an apprenticeship program. The continued growth and success, even through the recession of 2008-2011, enabled the property to be paid for in full by December 2010. The only hiccup was the nature of the location. A full 35 minutes drive from Hillsboro, a suburb of Portland, where there was quality shopping and recreational and educational activities for the four kids, left a feeling of isolation and seclusion. It was especially hard on Rumiko, as many of the friends she had come to know and grow close to were living in or near Hillsboro. I asked Rumiko if she would like to search for a house, closer to Hillsboro. Of course, a new house would have to have provisions for a shop and enough land to feel spacious as well as be within a determined budget. Rumiko took to researching property on the Internet with gusto.

For six months Rumiko scoured the 'net, but one evening in October I happened across a "For Sale" sign. The owners were home and courteously invited me in to visit. The property seemed perfect. Actually, Rumiko had spied this property, but had given up on it without further investigation because of the apparent lack of a shop facility. But that just turned out to be a gross omission in the realtor's ad, when in fact a huge shop facility was already in place. As soon as we saw it together, we made an offer. Soon we were fully moved in, including a newer shop in newly renovated shop space.

Evolution of the Carter Cutlery Business Model

The current successful business model for Carter Cutlery has been shaped by every last bit of exposure I have had to business during 41 years of life. I have been blessed to learn from my mistakes, and to eventually humble myself by seeking counsel from those who already experienced success. If you follow my tips, keep in mind that the best you can hope to do is to do your best. I claim that in business, a person's best effort is always good enough. I traveled a bumpy road and paid a high price for my current business success. Along the journey I found out the true meaning of success and it was quite different from what I had originally set out to achieve. Without seeking after the first, I doubt I would have discovered the second.

Once I started to attend knife shows in 1998, I jumped in with both feet. I researched as many shows as I could find out about, and tried to attend as many of them as I could, in Japan, in the U.S. and France. This exposure to the world's custom knife makers and the prices they got for their knives proved to be one of the best guides for me to accurately assess the appeal, demand and value of my work. I kept incrementally increasing my prices over the years until I noticed I no longer heard the constant comment that my prices were too low. I tempered that with a survey of how many knives I sold to repeat customers. I was happy to find a high percentage (approximately 30 percent) of repeat customers at knife shows, which validated to me that a satisfied customer would buy a second kitchen knife or outdoor knife even if the price was more expensive than the first.

Murray sharpening knives free-hand at a knife show.

A great blessing for Carter Cutlery emerged out of the knife show circuit. Because I am so obsessed with the metallurgical quality of my knives, and especially the condition of their cutting edges for which Japanese knives are known, I felt compelled to personally hand-sharpen each and every knife before I sold it to the customer. My simple sharpening stones traveled with me to every show I went to. During the show, I would draw a large crowd as I skillfully held a stone in one hand and a blade in the other and put a free hand "scary sharp" edge on a blade in under a minute or two.

As exciting as that was, it was the running narration and the simple explanation that amazed the crowds. Never before had the crowd seen sharpening demonstrated and explained in such simple, common sense terms. It made sense to them. Gone were the mystique, the confusion and ineffective instructions. I would actually dull a knife on purpose, and then let the crowd examine the blade edge each time I demonstrated one of the six steps of sharpening. After the crowd had felt the edge several different times, in about five minutes, from dull to scary sharp, they were convinced of two things: sharpening can be easy, and Murray really knows how to teach!

Show after show I drew a crowd to my table and held their utmost attention and interest. Soon the demos and explanations branched out into other areas of blade-smithing. I was polishing my skills at taking seemingly complicated procedures and explaining and demonstrating them in ways that the average Joe could understand. I was becoming a bladesmithing teacher.

I have developed a comprehensive customer data base and commissioned a first-class web site. I learned that customers appreciate hearing from me and appreciate that I have exciting offers for them. I learned how to write exciting offers that benefit the customers. I now send out electronic newsletters and sales offers as often as I can. I have learned the importance of "positioning" to establish credibility, and to establish trust with customers.

I have developed a free promotional eight-minute "Shop Tour" DVD and produced a second DVD for sale called "Advanced Blade Sharpening Techniques." My unique bladesmithing school offers students rare traditional Japanese bladesmithing instruction in English, which is unavailable anywhere else in the world. In response to the increase in demand, I have raised my prices across the board and orders have still increased.

Web Site Development: Making Sales While You Sleep

For years in Japan I stubbornly resisted the advance of technology. I clung to old ideas of business being properly conducted face to face. It wasn't until the turn of the 21st century that I touched a computer. The first step was learning to use email. Fortunately, I wasn't too much of a relic to see the advantages of instant communication.

Even when I arrived in the United States in 2005, I was trying to justify my apprehension about creating a website. I reasoned that it would cost too much money and time to maintain it. On top of that, I was still making monthly payments on 10,000 copies of my 20-page color catalog, which cost $6,000.

Shamus, my apprentice of six years, learns proper forge maintenance.

I soon found out that while web development is expensive, ignorance is even more costly. The first lady who volunteered to produce a website for me quit half way through the project, taking $2,400 of my money and leaving me high and dry. Fortunately, a friend's wife with advanced computer skills took on the challenge of picking up where the other gal left off and completed my first site. Thanks Christy! It was a decent site for a first attempt, and we experienced our first on-line sales through this site. Tim McCalla, my assistant at that time, and I fondly recount the evening we first uploaded knives for sale with their descriptions. When we finally finished putting those few knives online, which seemed to take us forever, we clicked over to the shopping cart and were amazed to see three knives had sold already. We both felt like pinching ourselves because it felt so unreal.

A business aquaintance later introduced me to a top-notch website developer, Aston Sanders at www.websitesinaflash.com, and immediately we started working on a new and visually superior website, with a better-organized layout. Fortunately, we had a large selection of outstanding photography to choose from thanks to photographer Hiro Soga. The nifty thing about our new website was the new connection between our products and services for sale, payment options through PayPal and the ease of transfer of funds to and from our business bank account. We were literally selling product 24 hours a day, and the funds were being deposited right where we needed them.

Carter Cutlery Business Advice to Live By

- Decide what your product or service will be—find a need and you will find a way to provide a necessary product or service.
- Concentrate on the task at hand and fully devote yourself to learning everything you can about the subject of your choice.
- Have a plan—know where you want to go so that you minimize getting sidetracked.
- Stick to the plan—seek wise counsel, make a plan and don't give up until you have accomplished your goal. Then make the next plan.
- If you adopt and follow someone else's proven model for success, try to modify it to make it reflect who you are, or risk alienating your customers.
- Attend as many trade shows/conferences relevant to your product or service as possible, especially in the early years of your business. Ask lots of questions.
- Invest as much as possible back into marketing the business.
- Make it a policy to respond to all email and phone inquiries within 24 hours.
- Hire the best website developer you can afford.
- Hire the best accountant you can afford.
- Even if you are not computer savvy, learn how to do your own recordkeeping, such as with Quickbooks.
- Hire the best staff members you can afford.
- Study diligently the qualities a good leader: 1) honesty; 2) forward thinking; 3) competency; and 4) inspirational.
- Delight in serving others.
- Be true to your faith and continually give thanks for your successes.
- Don't be afraid to take chances and try new things—you will learn from your mistakes and profit from the few successful innovations.
- Avoid borrowing money as if your reputation, family life, savings account and future are on the line, because they are.
- Even if you have to wait twice as long to begin a project while you save the cash, you will finish the project in three times the speed.
- Be a list-maker and each morning start with the least appealing task and get that done first. Everything else will be easier now.
- Don't worry or fret. Trust in the fact that your very best effort will always be good enough.

- Expect setbacks. You can turn them into a success by simply working through them with a smile.
- Surpass customer expectations—under-promise and over-deliver.
- Have integrity—keep your word and do what you say you will do.
- Develop a detailed customer base—it is much easier to sell to customers who are already interested in what you offer.
- Focus on the question, "How can I make it better?" rather than obsessing about perfection.
- To remain effective, you need weekly rest. Don't work more than six days a week.
- The best insurance you can have is a good diet and regular exercise.
- Try life without drugs, alcohol, caffeine and stress.
- Pay your bills on time, especially to your suppliers— they are keeping you in business.

In summary, take one day at a time. Keep moving forward. Setbacks must be seen as opportunities, and how you deal with those can determine if those, also, count as forward motion. Rest when your body tells you to, and remember that very few things in business are a matter of life and death. If you need spiritual strength, open a bible. If you don't have one, ask me for one of mine. To read my personal testimony of faith, go to www.carter-cutlery.com/testimony.

Inroads Into Japanese Hearts

As mentioned, I am the only Caucasian ever recognized as a Japanese bladesmithing master, who speaks and reads the Japanese language fluently, and who has been gifted in the area of communicating with the native Japanese to a degree that is rare in any industry.

I have had a fascination with Japan, its culture, crafts and people, since my early days in high school. I read and researched as much as I could. I immersed myself in karate, then the language, sushi making, traditional bladesmithing, motor sports, taiko drums and hunting. I studied and took tests in the native language in topics such as metallurgy, welding, history, hang-gliding, sign language, gun ownership and hunting.

All those rich experiences helped me communicate with the Japanese, but there was something else that got me "inside." I believe the great strides I made while living there were a result of the pure and simple love that I have for the Japanese people. I have an incredible sense of indebtedness to and respect for them. On a recent trip to Japan, after six years absence, upon reuniting with friends and acquaintances, I felt my relationship with most of them had grown closer, and not more distant. When I ask about trade secrets of fellow bladesmiths in Japan, it usually doesn't even occur to me that they wouldn't answer my questions. When the question is asked in the right spirit, and the proper reverence is shown when the question is graciously answered, an even stronger bond forms between me and my colleague. It's all about sincerity. I sense my life path is heading towards an even more meaningful relationship with the Japanese people.

Okay, Let's Get Started

The materials presented herein are intended to guide the reader through the complex process of forging and completion of the highest quality blades possible. There are many approaches to bladesmithing. This is the approach and technique of Carter Cutlery, the result of studying traditional bladesmithing for over 24 years, 18 in Japan and six in the U.S., perfecting the techniques via 16,000 completed forged blades.

There are two ways to learn something new – by reading and by doing. Learning how to forge blades favors the doing approach, but a combined study can accelerate the learning curve. Take every opportunity you can to light a fire, heat some steel and hammer away at it for the most effective study possible. Reading after that should be used as a tool to confirm that what you did was either correct, or needing corrections. Each successive experience in the forge will render lessons evident by no other means. You will get better with each attempt.

In general there are two approaches to making knives – the precision method and the eyeball approach. The precision method involves learning to use and employing calipers, surface grinders, height gages, lathes and milling machines. If a bladesmith wishes to make folding knives, this approach is usually necessary. A more artistic approach is to eyeball all measurements. I have developed a unique approach to bladesmithing called micro observation. This approach, which is well within the abilities of most students, relies on the wonderful ability of the naked eye to see precisely every detail of the workpiece when examined properly. Superior problem diagnosis, which is a combination of micro observation and seasoned discretion, can result in knives that can truly be considered a precision work of art. Through the practice of this method, I regularly teach students to trust their eyes and their discretion to make superior blades. Consequently, many of the techniques included in this book rely on good eyesight and a disciplined, patient heart.

As a general rule, try to make everything in duplicate. This will allow you valuable repetition and a chance to develop muscle memory. Another rule is this: no matter how difficult the project and no matter what setbacks you experience along the way, stick with it until the blade is completed. The steel is not the only thing being forged during this process.

I leave you with these quotes to ponder:

"What you have learned from others you will quickly forget. What you have learned with your whole body you will remember for the rest of your life." Ginchin Funakoshi, Karate Master

"If the job is once begun, don't leave the task until it's done. Be the labor great or small, do it well or not at all." From an old friend

"Some people dream of success...while others wake up and work hard at it." Author Unknown

"Through wisdom a house is built, and by understanding it is established. By knowledge the rooms are filled, with all precious and pleasant riches." Pro 24:3,4

Dangers In The Bladesmith Shop

CHAPTER 1

Sakamoto Shiki (Sakamoto Type)
Power Belt Hammer.

No doubt you will be tempted to skip this chapter and move on to the next. I don't blame you; I have done that occasionally when I wanted to 'get moving' into the heart of a book, and considered myself invincible anyway. So I will ease the burden here by giving you a realistic warning on each of the dangerous pieces of equipment we use when making knives. I won't tell you that you could be maimed for life from using a pair of vise-grips, or any other unrealistic warning. I'll just tell you what I have experienced or seen, and the damage that I have imagined each tool could do if an accident occurred.

Power hammer

I have never hurt myself with a power hammer, even after forging more than 16,000 blades with it. Sometimes I can feel the front spring section moving very close to my head as I'm forging, but I don't envision an injury, barring some unforeseen force lifting me up and throwing me into the front of the moving power hammer. In-

Cut off hardie in the hardie hole of the anvil.

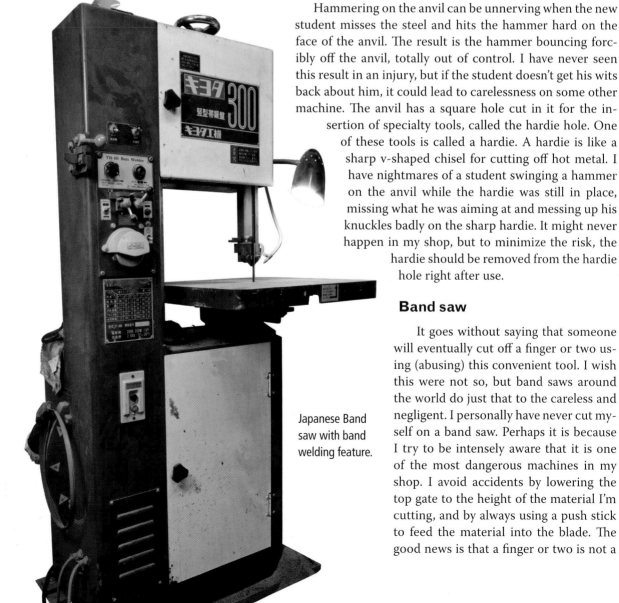

Japanese Band saw with band welding feature.

cidentally, if my foot comes off the hammer's foot pedal, the hammer will stop anyway. Many people comment, when they first see the hammer in action, that they would hate to get a finger or hand between the top and bottom dies as it is moving. That would indeed be unsightly, but so far, everybody has managed to refrain from the temptation. I would be surprised if it ever happens. (I know, I know. Someone, somewhere will prove me wrong!)

The power hammer is indeed powerful and intimidating to those who have not used it, but in the end, does not have a track record of danger.

Cut-off hardie in the anvil

Hammering on the anvil can be unnerving when the new student misses the steel and hits the hammer hard on the face of the anvil. The result is the hammer bouncing forcibly off the anvil, totally out of control. I have never seen this result in an injury, but if the student doesn't get his wits back about him, it could lead to carelessness on some other machine. The anvil has a square hole cut in it for the insertion of specialty tools, called the hardie hole. One of these tools is called a hardie. A hardie is like a sharp v-shaped chisel for cutting off hot metal. I have nightmares of a student swinging a hammer on the anvil while the hardie was still in place, missing what he was aiming at and messing up his knuckles badly on the sharp hardie. It might never happen in my shop, but to minimize the risk, the hardie should be removed from the hardie hole right after use.

Band saw

It goes without saying that someone will eventually cut off a finger or two using (abusing) this convenient tool. I wish this were not so, but band saws around the world do just that to the careless and negligent. I personally have never cut myself on a band saw. Perhaps it is because I try to be intensely aware that it is one of the most dangerous machines in my shop. I avoid accidents by lowering the top gate to the height of the material I'm cutting, and by always using a push stick to feed the material into the blade. The good news is that a finger or two is not a matter of life or death, and I bet doctors would have no trouble putting them back on.

Abrasive cut-off circular saw

This is the tool that claims ownership to the first scar I got from blade-smithing. Used the way it was designed to be used, it couldn't cut you in a thousand years. Ah, but I found another way to use this machine that has saved me hundreds of hours over the years, profiling forged blades. Before I learned to be careful and to wear leather gloves, I pushed my left index finger into the moving blade which resulted in a scar I can see to this day. No stitches were necessary. Only a little pain and hurt pride. I do know a bladesmith in Japan who pushed a little harder than I did and was hurt a little worse. In reality, sparks in the eye pose a greater danger, and so eye protection is a must with the circular cut-off wheel.

Abrasive cut off wheel.

Below: Two of the three drill presses used at Carter Cutlery.

Drill press

The drill press is, fortunately, nothing like a lathe. The drill presses in my shop will not twist around a glove, pull your finger off and rip your forearm muscles from the bones like a lathe will. What can be dangerous is if the drill bit catches a piece of sharp metal (a knife?) as the hole breaks through the other side and starts to spin the whole piece. I have found that if I hold on really tight (yes, I hand hold every piece of metal that I drill, if it is long enough to hold) this won't happen. The drill stalls out before the piece rips out of your hand. I guess my drill presses are wimpy, I can't vouch for yours. I will say that if I had to clamp every piece I've drilled in a vise, I'd still be working on the 3000th knife and not the 17,000th. The only injury from the drill press was from a curly nickel silver filing scratching my left hand producing a trickle of blood.

Grinders

Belt grinders, in general, look fiercer than they are. The worst I have seen is a bit of ground fingernail or a little bit of skin removed. It sure smarts and takes a while to heal, but isn't very serious in the overall scheme of things. There is the danger of getting a finger caught between the belt and a contact wheel, which would likely result in a broken finger, but I have not seen it.

Three of the five belt grinders used ay Carter Cutlery.

Long arbor buffing wheels and flap sanders.

Cement base stone on the left and new epoxy base stone on the right.

The exception is the bench grinder. Folks, my bench grinder is huge, and care must be taken to never put a finger near the platen and the moving wheel. The platen must be constantly adjusted so that there is almost no space between it and the wheel. A good friend of mine caught his right hand index finger in his bench grinder (half the size of mine) and it tore all of the meat off of his finger.

All the grinders produce dust and sparks, so eye protection is mandatory.

Buffing wheels

Buffing wheels will occasionally catch the object being buffed (when held at the wrong angle to the wheel) and launch it at high speeds. If the launched object happens to be a knife, the problem is magnified. If it is flying at someone else or yourself, it won't be pretty. Several knifemakers have launched a blade into their thigh or stomach from the buffer. It has not happened to me, yet. Holding the blade to be buffed at the right position (remember that Carter Cutlery buffers rotate away from the bladesmith) will eliminate 99 percent of the risk, and holding it at the right angle will prevent the other one percent. Holding the blade securely puts the odds in your favor as well. Never let another person get down range of where you buff.

Kaiten toishi (rotating water stones)

I have suffered the most stitches (only seven stitches) and pain while using this machine. I don't think the machine itself is a mechanical liability, but the combination of cold water (in the winter) and fatigue has left its mark on me. Being careful and not working to the point of exhaustion could have prevented my accidents. The stone itself has agged corners, and when I slip and push my hand into the corner of the 400rpm moving stone, it is very painful. It does not break skin or bone, but boy does it ever smart. The stitches came when I was an apprentice. It was wintertime and the water to cool the stone was freezing cold. My fingers were going numb as I was sharpening a sushi knife (a Yanagi-ba). I let my mind wander ...and now I have a nice scar on my left thumb. To add insult to injury, I didn't have health insurance and the doctor charged me a fortune to sew me up. All things considered though, not a bad track record for having sharpened more than 50,000 blades on these stones.

Welder

An electric stick or MIG welder is a valuable asset in the bladesmith shop. The real danger is the ultraviolet and infrared ray exposure to the skin, which will cause a bad sun burn and can lead to cancer. Make sure all of your body, including your hands, is covered. Little welding berries can strike you and cause a pencil-point sized first degree burn also. Proper ventilation is important when welding.

Molten flux from forge welding

When forge welding, the molten flux will fly out from the yellow hot billet of steel in every direction. It doesn't usually fly upwards, rather, out and down. Leather gloves, sleeves and apron are nice, but you'll get burned anyway. It's important to wear cotton clothes so that they will just smolder and not catch on fire. Getting a berry of molten flux in my shoe has to be one of the most memorable forge welding scars that I have. If you get burned while welding a billet of steel under the power hammer, you must forge on and let the hot berry extinguish itself in your flesh. Stopping what you are doing won't help anyway, you will ruin the steel and waste a lot of hard work. Once the forge welded piece is completed and the beautiful blade is in your hand, you will forget about the pain you experienced.

Bocashi (rotating brass wire wheel)

This is a common machine in rural Japanese bladesmith shops, but a novelty outside of Japan. Originally designed to finish the polished secondary edge of a mild steel/carbon steel laminate blade. It consists of a rotating wire brush, usually made of fine brass wire, which picks up a special mud slurry from the trough in which it rotates. The wire/mud combination gives the mild steel a cloudy look while the hardened carbon steel resists the abrasion and stays shiny and polished. The contrast is stark. During the post war years in Japan, circa 1946, when high quality carbon steel was scarce, the bo-

MIG (Metal Inert Gas) electric welder. Note that Murray should be wearing gloves to protect his hands. Oops!

Molten flux from forge welding. At proper forge welding temperature, there will be few sparks coming from the steel.

Left: Bocashi rotating wire brush machine.

Center: Using vise grips to remove a handle pin.

Right: Caution: Very Hot!

cashi allowed the smith to show his customers just how much steel he was using in his blades.

I have never injured myself with this little tool, but it is possible that a strand of brass wire could come flying at your eye. The solution: eye protection.

Cleaning hundreds of blades at a time can leave the skin on your fingertips a little thin too. Not likely to happen to you.

Hand tools

Hand tools, ranging from files to pliers to screwdrivers and wrenches, could all become dangerous if one is careless or negligent. I have had no injuries that I can remember with hand tools (although I am apt to pinch my fleshy hands in the handles of a certain pair of tin snips from time to time). Wood chisels require an extra amount of caution, but are rarely used in the bladesmith shop.

Below: Hammer, anvil and tongs: the most used tools in the bladesmith shop.

Forge/hot coals

From time to time, a newly added piece of coke will contain some moisture and will audibly pop in the fire. Parts of it can fly out the front of the forge where the smith is standing. As a result, after adding a scoop of fresh coke to the fire, don't choose that time to scrutinize the inside of the forge...a hot piece of coke could come flying at your face. On the other hand, red hot coals that

drop out of the fire can usually be safely picked up briefly and put back in the forge if the smith has leather gloves on. Even with bare hands, a red hot coal can be moved or whisked away in an emergency without getting burned, if the motion is fast enough.

Above: Steam coming from this hot blade shows its true temperature despite the lack of glowing color.

Hot metal

If a piece of really hot metal is set down in bright light, it may not look hot to the unknowing. If someone grasps it, they will be burned quite badly. The smart thing to do in the bladesmith shop is hold your hand at least an inch away from a piece of steel to ascertain whether it is hot or not. I've burned myself several times, but never seriously. Leather gloves will protect your hands somewhat from hot steel, but NEVER let those gloves get wet and then handle hot steel, or you will give your hands a steam bath they will never forget.

Below: Hold on tight.

Handling sharp knives

At a certain point in the knife-making process, it becomes necessary to grind an edge on the blade. If you have to hold that blade in your hand, for example, while you are grinding/sanding the handle, the trick is to hold the blade tightly. If you hold it tightly then the blade can't move laterally in your hand. If it cannot move, it will not cut you. Some tape the knife edges and some don't bother to sharpen their knives (ever!). However, in order to finish the knife completely, at some point

during the finishing process it needs an edge that you can see. I hold on to razor sharp knives all the time in this manner and have never received a cut that needed stitches.

The really nasty machines: hydraulic and mechanical flywheel presses

I don't use hydraulic or flywheel presses in my shop. They are excellent time savers and an incredibly efficient machine for industry, but they MAIM FOR LIFE. Every severely deformed hand and finger of my bladesmithing brothers has been caused by these beasts. Not for me, thank you very much!

Use of safety gear: When, where and why

Safety glasses

Safety glasses are required for most dangerous activities, and it would be easy to say "Wear your safety glasses at all times when in the bladesmith shop." However, there are times when wearing

Below: Dust mask, goggles and ear protection will keep you breathing, seeing and hearing for years to come.

them is not practical because they interfere with some blademaking operations. As a guideline, always wear them around machines that produce sparks. Some will choose to wear them when they forge metal, by hand or with the power hammer. I choose not to, against well-wishers' best warnings. I have my reasons, after forging 16,000 blades, which make sense to me. For the new bladesmith: when in doubt, put them on.

Dust mask or respirator

The occasional trip to the blademith shop is not likely to give you lung cancer, but constant exposure to metal dust, exotic wood dust, coke and charcoal dust absolutely will. Historically, blacksmiths and bladesmiths succumbed to many lung ailments. Use your mask for light grinding/forging tasks, and a respirator when doing serious grinding.

Eye goggles can save your sight. Here I use a modified pick-axe tagane to dress the rotating water stone.

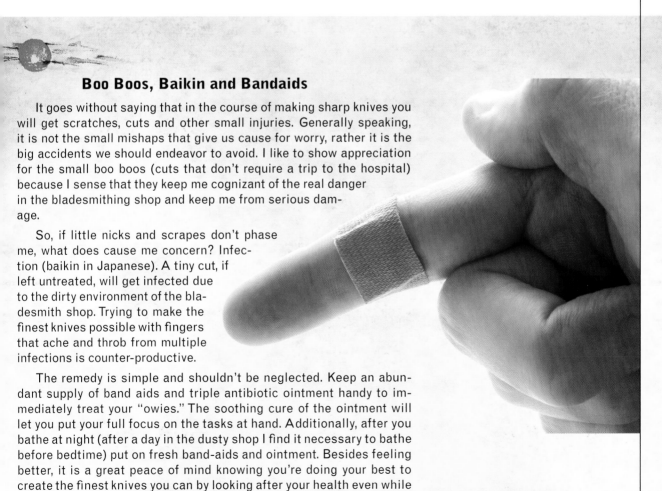

Boo Boos, Baikin and Bandaids

It goes without saying that in the course of making sharp knives you will get scratches, cuts and other small injuries. Generally speaking, it is not the small mishaps that give us cause for worry, rather it is the big accidents we should endeavor to avoid. I like to show appreciation for the small boo boos (cuts that don't require a trip to the hospital) because I sense that they keep me cognizant of the real danger in the bladesmithing shop and keep me from serious damage.

So, if little nicks and scrapes don't phase me, what does cause me concern? Infection (baikin in Japanese). A tiny cut, if left untreated, will get infected due to the dirty environment of the blademith shop. Trying to make the finest knives possible with fingers that ache and throb from multiple infections is counter-productive.

The remedy is simple and shouldn't be neglected. Keep an abundant supply of band aids and triple antibiotic ointment handy to immediately treat your "owies." The soothing cure of the ointment will let you put your full focus on the tasks at hand. Additionally, after you bathe at night (after a day in the dusty shop I find it necessary to bathe before bedtime) put on fresh band-aids and ointment. Besides feeling better, it is a great peace of mind knowing you're doing your best to create the finest knives you can by looking after your health even while you are sleeping!

Practical Parameters
of Cutlery Design

As excited as you must be to get in the forge and start forging steel that will become a knife, don't waste your time, efforts and valuable materials by starting without a plan. In my advice for business I offered three pointers that will ensure your bladesmithing adventure is successful: 1) Have a plan. 2) Stick to the plan. 3) Concentrate on the task at hand. Lets examine all three before we discuss the nitty-gritty of designing knives.

Whether you are interested in bladesmithing as a hobby or as a profession, you will get the most satisfaction and fulfillment from your efforts when you actually complete the knives you set out to make. Bladesmithing is nothing more than an elaborate sequence of skillful steps that transform raw materials into a finished knife. Trying to forge and complete a knife without a plan is akin to painting a picture on a blank canvas without an image in your head to start with. There may be a few geniuses among us who could do just that, but I'm guessing that most of us will do much better with a plan.

Below: Starting point for knife sketch.

Knife "emerges" from pattern
of curved lines.

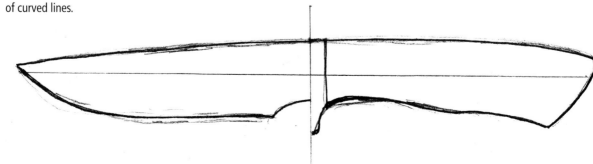

One eminently useful knife (neck knife) and another bound to sit at the bottom of a drawer for years on end! Big knives are cool and irreplaceable in a few survival circumstances, but for the most part will not see daily use.

The plan for forging a knife starts with a simple life-size sketch. If you have no idea where to start, you might browse through a cutlery catalog or surf the internet for inspiration. Once you have an idea of what you would like to sketch, get a white piece of paper big enough for your design, a ruler, a pencil and an eraser. Place the paper in front of you so that its long side is left to right, and not up and down. On the paper draw a straight line with the ruler left to right, and then a second line intersecting the first like a cross on its side. Everything on one side of the cross will become the blade and everything on the other will become the handle. The cross line can become the guard if your design calls for one. The long straight line will eventually be erased as it is only used for reference.

Use nice sweeping curves to draw the back of the spine of the knife flowing smoothly into the handle. As you sketch lines, don't erase any lines yet. Sketch as many lines as you feel necessary, until you can "see" your knife start to emerge. When the complete profile of the knife is in the sketch to your satisfaction, you can easily erase all the unwanted lines.

Now let's discuss some practical design elements and what to avoid if you are a beginner or intermediate level.

For a great reference point to start from, go to your kitchen and pick out

Knives reproduced faithfully from sketch will grow your skill and confidence.

Carter Cutlery patterns made from sheet metal.

the most comfortable knife there. That knife you are now holding probably comes close to what we would consider a practical design. Notice how certain features are conspicuously missing: no tanto points, no recurved blades, no fancy filework, no fancy finger grooves and no radical lines. You might notice how comfortable the handle is and how efficient the handle conveys the control from your hand to the cutting edge of the blade. Given that in the forge it would be exciting enough to faithfully copy that for a first knife, I suggest your design sketch look closer to that kitchen knife than something out of the movie "Fantastical Warriors from Another World."

Practical blade length is another factor to consider. While many men see a knife as a possible weapon that we could use to chop our way out of a zombie mob, the truth is that most EDC (Every Day Carry) knives have blades about three inches long. Deer and elk hunters might be able to use four inches, but very few knives benefit from longer blades. A five inch blade might not sound like a problematic modification, but very few five inch bladed knives are ever pressed into daily service. If a chopper is desired, don't mess with a five or six inch blade, just go straight to an eight or nine inch minimum.

A common mistake of new knifemakers is to make the handle too short. When sketching the handle, if in doubt, err on the long side. Revisit the kitchen again and examine the handles on knives you consider comfortable. EDC knives are held in the hand in all possible grip configurations, so allow for freedom of movement.

Once you have settled on a knife design, be sure to trace the line with a dark pencil, and then glue the paper to some stiff single sheet cardboard, such as the kind that cold cereal boxes are made of. Make sure the whole

Collecting Blade Patterns

One of the greatest assets a professional blade-smith will accumulate is a large collection of useful and popular patterns. One way to acquire a new pattern is to draw it out on paper and then glue it to cardboard, The cardboard pattern is then faithfully scribed on to a thin, straight sheet of metal, thin steel being the best for longevity and ease of modification. The pattern is then cut or ground out faithfully, constantly comparing the original to the new pattern.

Another way to acquire a new pattern is to copy another bladesmith's patterns with permission. This is a big favor to receive, so expect to do something kind in return!

One way to get new knife patterns that has worked great for me is the "innovation" method. I make, for example, 20 copies of the same knife, but when I am cold forging them and grinding out the profile, I'll have a little fun with the lines. I'll extend a line here, cut into a line there, and end up with twenty knives that look similar, but are not exact copies. Inevitably, one knife will stand out from all the others as being "just right." If you like that version, immediately copy it on to thin sheet metal so that you will have a pattern to reproduce in the future. Don't make my past mistake of believing you can recreate the exact same knife again from memory, because you probably won't be able to do it. This copy may give birth to another version in the future, and eventually, by this method alone, you will accumulate many patterns.

Now this will be of interest for the bladesmith who aspires to earn a full time income from blade-smithing. Obviously, not all patterns will be popular. I have, in the past, poured out my heart designing a knife that seemed to have all the "right stuff" and yet wouldn't sell until I lowered the price considerably. On the other hand, I have models of knives that literally sell like hot cakes. Make note of which patterns sell the best, and be sure to always have a stock of that model on hand for a good cash flow. Once you have a healthy number of the "best sellers" in stock ready for immediate delivery, you can have fun experimenting with new designs.

Above: Paper patterns reproduced in sheet metal for posterity.

Below: Early Carter Cutlery offerings in neck knives, many showing similar pedigree, circa 1998.

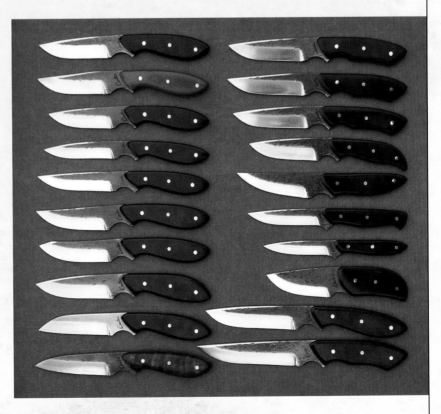

Ladder pattern Damascus Whitecrane knife.

pattern is glued down tight so that when you later cut it out parts of the pattern won't be flapping back and forth. When the glue is dry cut the pattern out with a very sharp knife or pair of scissors. Now you have a template for the knife you will make. The ultimate goal is to make a faithful reproduction of your template in steel. No changing the design half way through! Once you have done this successfully, you'll gain the confidence that will allow you to reproduce anything in steel that you can draw on paper.

The Magic of a Millimeter

There is a stark contrast in what drives sales between culinary knives for the kitchen and leisure knives for hobbies, such as hunting, pocket, camping and survival knives. I like to say that 90 percent of the influence for a kitchen knife sale is based on the bladesmith's reputation for cutting performance and only 10 percent based on aesthetics. Conversely, for hobby knives the decision is based primarily (90 percent) on aesthetics and only 10 percent on the maker's reputation.

The conclusion from the above statement is that if you decide to make culinary knives for a living, you had better concentrate on delivering superior cutting and maintenance performance in your blades. Making them stylistic and fancy can come later once you have attained excellent metallurgy. With hobby knives however, producing knives that look awesome should be your first goal. If a customer saw ten knives on a table and one of them was yours, you want your knife to be picked up first. Achieving this is very tough in the custom knife world. This is because the whole "essence" of a knife can change within the span of a millimeter.

When grinding the profile of a knife before heat treat and after when you are finishing it up, pay super attention to the profile lines, thinking in terms of millimeters. An extra millimeter in the belly of the blade can make the blade look "fat" and grinding a millimeter too much off the end of the handle can make the handle look "stubby." It really is amazing to see

Damascus International Pro Series Funayuki.

Jim's Knife. Damascus blade and mammoth ivory handle scales.

577 layer damascus yanagi-ba with ironwood handle and saya with ivory and silver nickel fittings.

Blade Patterns in Traditional Japanese Cutlery

One significant difference between western cutlery and Japanese cutlery is that Japanese cutlery tends to be much more task-specific. I was surprised that most domestic kitchens I visited in Japan had at least three or four task-specific blades on hand, varying vastly in shape and thickness. These blades appeared to get constant use and were almost always sharp enough to slice paper. On the other hand, we see the wooden block with knives on North American kitchen counters, with several knives very similar in shape and thickness, only varying in their size and length. It is also sad to point out that rarely are any of them fit for cutting.

Perhaps an explanation for this difference is that, historically, Japanese people moved around their country much less frequently than here in North America. Because there was less need to pack up and transport ones belongings, it was easier to own and store a greater variety of task specific tools. In North America however, our history is of constant moving and relocation, and necessity dictated that one knife be used for as many tasks as possible. As a result, even though affluence allows us to purchase a greater number of knives, they tend to be similar in shape and function.

It is still common for Japanese housewives to shop for food daily and prepare various fresh foods for the evening meal. Kitchen knives are put to the test every day in this environment. Conversely, in North America, shopping may be done only once a week, and in some cases only once a month. (This trend is not followed by some groups of "Foodies" who lean more towards daily preparation of fresh produce.) Emphasis is placed upon convenience and processed foods are the standard fare. Many groceries purchased for the average North American home do not even need the use of a knife before eating.

Another explanation that sheds some light on the various shapes of Japanese cutlery is how they prepare their food. Traditional Japanese cuisine places much importance on freshness and, more often than not, food is eaten raw. Many of their knife designs facilitate minimal damage to delicate food. Two knives that stand out are the "kata-ha nakiri" and "yanagi-ba." In contrast, western cooking involves more processing and cooking where the quality of the cut is not as important as in Japanese cuisine.

As a result of the demands of Japanese consumers, Japanese bladesmiths field a vast array of cutlery to choose from. In fact, nowhere in the world exists as diverse a selection of

From Left to Right: Deba, funayuki, nakiri, wabocho and yanagi-ba.

kitchen knives as in Japan. Of the literally hundreds of designs found in the archipelago, five basic blade patterns emerge as the most common. They are the deba-bocho, funayuki-bocho, nakiri-bocho, wabocho (santoku), and yanagi-ba (sashimi-bocho).

The deba-bocho with its massively thick and heavy blade is primarily for cutting whole fish apart, something that is still commonly done in the average domicile in Japan. The deba is also put to use when the cutting chore would be too taxing for either one of the thin blades on hand. Debas with a blade length around 165mm are the easiest to use, and interestingly, a smaller deba called ko-deba (less than135mm) is considered a real expert's blade and takes considerable skill in its proper use.

The wabocho is the workhorse of domestic Japanese cuisine. It is characterized by a very wide and thin blade and an abrupt point. Most wabocho average about 160mm in blade length. One of the wabocho's desirable features is that, due to the wide blade, it can be repeatedly sharpened over many years and still retain its usefulness.

sun deba in ironwood and black micarta

The funayuki is a variation on the wabocho, in that it too has a very thin blade. The graceful isosceles-shaped blade is pointier and a little narrower in width than the wabocho. A funayuki-bocho can vary widely in length from 105-240mm in blade length, and sometimes even longer. The funayuki, literally meaning "boat (ocean) going," is actually a hybrid between a wabocho and a yanagi-ba. It was designed to take aboard fishing vessels where the fisherman could cut up some of the catch for immediate tasting to verify the quality of the fish. Being shorter than a real yanagi-ba, it was easier to use and store on the confined space of a fishing vessel. Smaller funayuki blades (105-135mm) are often used in Japan like a paring knife is used in North America.

funayuki

The nakiri is the epitome of a vegetable cutting blade. It literally means "leaf cutter," and that really is the best description of this awesome tool. Generally they have very thin blades, but some of the professional kata-ha blades tend to be thicker. The average nakiri-bocho has a 165mm length blade. Unlike any of the other Japanese blades, only the nakiri will retain its original length after years of repeated sharpening, even though the blade will get narrower. Despite the absence of a pointy tip, the corner edge of the na- kiri heel is used to pierce packaging. Interestingly, the nakiri is the most popular cutlery to give to a newlywed couple as a gift because of the lack of a pointed tip. Well wishers are hoping that this will prevent it from becoming "exhibit A" after the couple has their first disagreement.

nakiri

The yanagi-ba is the raw fish (sashimi) connoisseur's blade of choice. It is designed so that a mouth-sized piece of fish can be rendered with just one smooth drawing slice of the knife. The yanagi should be drawn towards the user, and never used in a sawing back and forth motion. Consequently, yanagi-ba blades tend to be the longest common blades, with most between 240-300mm.

wabocho

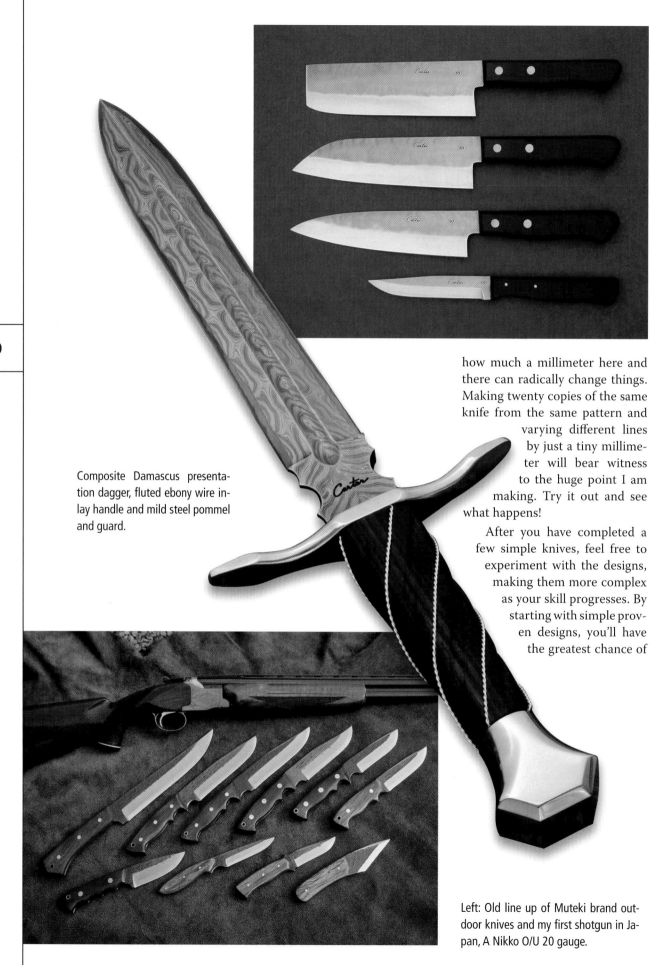

Composite Damascus presentation dagger, fluted ebony wire inlay handle and mild steel pommel and guard.

how much a millimeter here and there can radically change things. Making twenty copies of the same knife from the same pattern and varying different lines by just a tiny millimeter will bear witness to the huge point I am making. Try it out and see what happens!

After you have completed a few simple knives, feel free to experiment with the designs, making them more complex as your skill progresses. By starting with simple proven designs, you'll have the greatest chance of

Left: Old line up of Muteki brand outdoor knives and my first shotgun in Japan, A Nikko O/U 20 gauge.

actually completing the knife, which will build both your skill and confidence. Never lose sight of the fact that the ultimate goal of bladesmithing is to make a blade of superior metallurgy that performs better than any other knife on the market. Never be concerned with the visual appearance of a knife to the point where you lose sight of the main goal.

And now, (finally!) let's get into the exciting process of forging and completing high performance cutlery.

Medium weight kama sickle.

Selection of Steel

Hot steel ready for forging.

There are three approaches to selecting steel for the purpose of forging blades.

The first approach: Research

The first and most logical approach is to select steel by doing some research on cutlery grade steel. Topics to especially pay attention to are the chemical composition of different steels and the effects of each chemical; isothermal transformation graphs for different steels; the effects and importance of thermal cycles, including annealing, quenching and tempering; the availability and cost of the steels and, perhaps most importantly, how easy the steels are to work by hand.

The above paragraph only took a few lines to write and a few minutes to compose, and yet many metallurgists will spend their whole lives researching those points. Pursue it to your heart's content, and to that end I have included a thorough bibliography at the back of this book. However, to get you focused back on the task at hand, suffice it to say that there are some specifics you will need to concentrate on when selecting steel. These are:

+ The amount of carbon in the steel
+ Forging temperature range
+ Annealing temperature, quenching temperature and tempering temperature
+ Availability
+ Overall workability

Let's examine each of these in a little more detail.

Carbon is added to iron (Fe) to make steel. Carbon is the element that enables steel to harden when it is quenched at the proper temperature. Steel is unique in this aspect; all other metals soften when subjected to the same thermal cycle. The amount of carbon is very important. Too little carbon will fail to make steel harden when quenched, and too much carbon turns cutlery steel into cast steel. Generally speaking, less than 0.5 percent carbon is considered low carbon steel, and not suitable for blades. More than 1.6 percent carbon is considered extremely high carbon steel, and is very tricky to make into a blade. More than two percent usually equates to cast steel. Hence, most blades in the world have a carbon content between 0.5 percent and 1.5 percent. In this range, all other factors being equal, the more carbon, the harder the blade gets when quenched. The harder the blade, the finer an edge and the longer it will stay sharp.

Forging temperature range is the temperature at which you can "work" or manipulate the steel. Most steel can be worked between a bright red heat and orange/yellow heat (approx .700~900 degrees Celsius, 1290-1650 Fahrenheit) and it will yield under the blow of the hammer, bend or twist etc.. Below this range the steel will cease to yield to manipulation and can be damaged by subjecting it to stress. Likewise, steel can be irreversibly damaged from working it at too high a temperature.

Sources of scrap steel, such as leaf springs, axles and old files.

Annealing, quenching and tempering are the three phases of heat treating steel. These temperatures are very critical figures to commit to memory for the steel you are working. The heart and soul of a blade is the heat treat, as the final quality of the blade will be determined by how successfully these three operations are accomplished. Knowing the proper temperatures, and knowing what they look and feel like, is a critical skill for the bladesmith.

Availability determines whether or not you will be able to try forging that 'super-steel' you have been reading about. If you cannot locate or buy the steel in question, the pursuit becomes meaningless. Cost is another factor. Even if you locate the steel of your dreams, it may cost too much to have it shipped to your location. You want to know if you can acquire the steel for a reasonable cost and if it will be available in the foreseeable future.

Overall workability considers how the steel in question compares to other steels. Is it easy to manipulate under the hammer when you are forging it? How does it heat treat? Is it prone to warping, bending or cracking? Is it easy to straighten after heat treating? How does it take a final polish? These questions are easier to answer once you have experience with a few of the common steels.

The second approach: Recycle

The second approach is to recycle steel and try to forge blades from whatever material can be procured. This is the cheapest way to get started forging cutlery, and can be downright exciting as well. If you still get excited by wrapped Christmas presents and are apt to buy lottery tickets, this approach may appeal to you. There can be incredible fulfillment and satisfaction in creating a useful tool from a long forgotten piece of steel. On the other hand, there can be a lot of frustration; for example, the blade comes out of the quenching medium cracked or twisted like a corkscrew because the steel was of "unknown" composition. Almost all bladesmiths will try this approach at least once during their career.

The third approach: Splurge

The third approach is simply to select the very best cutlery steel in the world for forging. The best is called Yasuki Hagane, and is made by a

Yasuki Steel Facility, Shimane, Japan.

subsidiary of Hitachi Metal Works in Yasuki City, Shimane Prefecture, Japan. The Yasuki steels that we usually encounter in the hand-forged blade world are a) White Steel b) Blue Steel or c) Blue Super Steel. Yasuki also markets a Yellow Steel, but it is not too common, and thus is mentioned in passing only.

White steel (1.2~1.4 percent carbon) is the flagship of Yasuki steel. It was born from the desire to engineer a steel that would mirror the ideals of Samurai sword legends. That is to say, a steel that was pure in chemical composition, would cut keener than any other steel before it, and would yield compliantly under the bladesmith's hammer. During the smelting process special attention is given to protecting the molten steel from pollutants such as phosphorous and sulfur. Apart from carbon and iron, there is little else to complicate this steel. Experienced Japanese bladesmiths praise white steel as the very best Japan has to offer the cutlery world. They believe that white steel is limited only by the skill, passion and devotion the smith brings to the forge with him. White steel is likened to a white canvas for a painter – void of any beauty until the skilled artist paints his masterpiece. White steel has some quirks that must be mastered before it will render a superior blade, and that is why only true masters can consistently produce superior knives in white steel.

Blue steel (1.2~1.4 percent carbon) is perhaps more commonly used than white steel in Japanese cutlery. Blue steel has white steel as its starting point, to which limited amounts of chromium (Cr), and tungsten (W) are added. These added elements serve to fundamentally change the internal structure of the steel from that of evenly dispersed spherical carbides (white steel) to star-like shaped, unevenly dispersed carbides. The result is steel that favors edge retention over the keenness of the cutting edge. Because blue steel is an "engineered" steel, the challenge for the smith is to forge and heat treat the steel in such a way as to not ruin any of the inherent qualities that are already in the steel. This takes markedly less experience to accomplish than does forging a superior blade from white steel. Hence, blue steel is favored by the wholesalers and thus more commonly found on the open market. Nevertheless, a

Chart of Yasuki steels.

YASUKI STEEL CHART									
	C	Si	Mn	P	S	Cr	Mo	V	W
Gokunantetsu	< 0.08	< 0.10	< 0.30	< 0.03	< 0.03				
S 25C	0.25	0.25	0.75	< 0.03	< 0.035				
Stainless Gokunantetsu	< 0.08	< 1.00	< 1.00	< 0.04	< 0.03	13.00			
Blue #1	1.20~1.40	0.10~0.20	0.20~0.30	< 0.025	< 0.004				1.50~2.00
Blue #2	1.00~1.20	0.10~0.20	0.20~0.30	< 0.025	< 0.004	0.20~0.50			1.50~2.00
White #1	1.20~1.40	0.10~0.20	0.20~0.30	< 0.025	< 0.004				
White #2	1.00~1.20	0.10~0.20	0.20~0.30	< 0.025	< 0.004				
Yellow #2	1.00~1.20	0.10~0.20	0.20~0.30	< 0.03	< 0.006				
Tansō Kōguko	1.00~1.10	< 0.35	< 0.50	< 0.03	< 0.03				
Tansō Kōguko	0.90~1.00	< 0.35	< 0.50	< 0.03	< 0.03				
Tansō Kōguko	0.80~0.90	< 0.35	< 0.50	< 0.03	< 0.03				
S 35C	0.35	0.25	0.75	< 0.03	< 0.035				
S 45C	0.45	0.25	0.75	< 0.03	< 0.035				
S 55C	0.55	0.25	0.75	< 0.03	< 0.035				
Blue Super	1.50	0.10~0.20	0.20~0.30	< 0.025	< 0.004	0.30~0.50	0.30~0.50	0.50	2.00~2.50

YASUKI STEELS, HEAT TREATING GUIDE LINES			
Steel	**Annealing Temp.**	**Quenching Temp.**	**Tempering Temp.**
White #1	740~770	760~800 water	180~220
White #2	740~770	760~800 water	180~220
Yellow #2	740~770	760~800 water	180~220
White #3	740~770	760~800 water 780~820 oil	180~220
Yellow #3	740~770	760~800 water 780~820 oil	180~220
Blue #1	750~780	780~830 water or oil	160~230
Blue #2	750~780	780~830 water or oil	160~230
Blue Super	750~780	780~830 water or oil	160~230
KK	740~770	780~830 oil	160~200
Gin 1	800~870	1040~1090 air or oil	100~150
Gin 3	800~870	1040~1090 air or oil	100~150
Gin 5	800~870	1040~1090 air or oil	100~150
All temperatures shown in degrees celcius. • To easily convert Celsius to Fahrenheit, multiply the figure in Celsius by 9, then divide by 5. Add 32 to get the figure in Fahrenheit. Just remember CF9532. • To convert from Fahrenheit to Celsius, subtract 32, multiply by 5 and then divide by 9. Just remember FC3259.			

skillfully-forged blade made from blue steel is still a marvel to behold and use.

Blue Super steel (1.5 percent carbon) was developed to push the performance envelope of the blue steel family. By adding 0.1 percent carbon and the elements vanadium (V) and molybdenum (Mo) a star was born. The added carbon and extra alloys make it the trickiest of the Yasuki steels to work with, but the results are astounding. Superior cutting and edge holding capabilities are achieved, making it come close to a great white steel blade, but not quite.

One common trait of White steel, Blue steel and Blue Super steel is the extremely high carbon content, between 1.2~1.5 percent. This results in steels that require very precise temperature control during forging and the heat treating process. Most other commercial cutlery grade carbon steels have less that 1.0 percent carbon, making those steels easier to forge, easier to heat treat and much more "forgiving" with respect to heating and cooling. If it weren't for the fact that these steels have as much as ten times the amount of pollutants, such as phosphorus and sulfur, they would make a fantastic entry level steel for the beginner to use.

At Carter Cutlery, the following specific temperatures are aimed for to achieve proper forging (F), annealing (A), quenching (Q) and tempering (T) temperatures. All temperatures shown represent degrees Celsius:

White steel...F...700~900, A...750, Q...790, T...180

Blue steel ....F...720~920, A...760, Q...810, T...200

Blue Super...F...720~920, A...760, Q...810, T...205

Metallurgy 101

Carbides are hard particles formed in steel, a compound of iron and carbon. Carbide type and size affect wear resistance and toughness. In steel carbides are found in various forms according to time and temperature: cementite, ferrite, austenite, martensite and pearlite.

Chart of Yasuki Steels, Heat Treating Guide Lines.

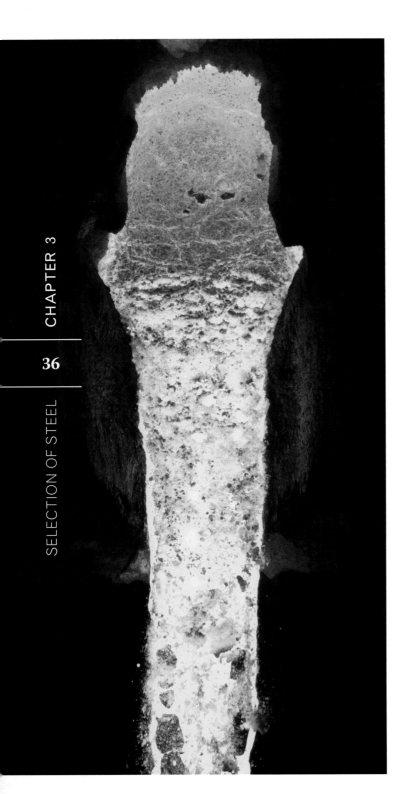

Grain size. Steel is made up of grains, and the grain size has an important effect on physical properties. At normal temperature, the smaller the grain size the stronger and harder the steel.

Wear resistance is the ability in steel to resist the loss of particles when in abrasive contact with other materials.

Strength means the steel's ability to resist deformation under applied forces.

Toughness is the steel's ability to absorb impact without fracturing. Generally strength and toughness are opposed to each other, raising the hardness lowers toughness. Only decreasing grain size increases both strength and toughness

Edge retention means the ability of a blade to hold an edge.

When choosing a steel for a knife, it is necessary to consider knife design, intended use, cost, ease of fabrication, edge holding ability, corrosion resistance, toughness, wear resistance and ease of sharpening. No one steel can meet all of these requirements perfectly. For example, the most wear resistant knife on the planet is going to be harder to sharpen and the most flexible knife will dull quickly. Knives for very specific applications must be made with steel that is appropriate for that application. There is no "One" tool steel that will provide all of the best qualities in all knives. Some trade-offs are necessary to achieve a quality knife that will perform the required task as expected.

Blade Hardness

A hard blade is the result of careful heat treating. Generally speaking, the harder the blade the better. With increased hardness, wear resistance (the ability of the blade to hold an edge) increases as does the keenness of the cutting edge. However, toughness is usually compromised by hardness, unless the steel and forging techniques you are using result in very fine grain structure. In knives, hardness is measured by the Rockwell C (Rc) scale which goes from 20-80. Most carbon steel blades are between Rc 52-58 and most stainless steel blades are between Rc 54-60. Hitachi Yasuki Hagane Steel when properly forged and heat-treated can attain a hardness of Rc 64 and still retain a useable level of toughness.

Alloying Elements

Carbon: not an alloying element, because it is present in all steels, but it is the most important hardening element. Increasing carbon increases hardness. It also increases the strength of steel but, added in isolation, decreases toughness. Blade steels are generally made of high carbon steel with at least .5 percent carbon content.

Chromium: improves corrosion resistance, wear resistance and hardenability. Steel with at least 13 percent chromium is generally deemed "stainless" steel. Adding chromium in high amounts decreases toughness.

Cobalt: improves strength and hardness, and permits quenching in higher temperatures. It also intensifies the individual effects of other elements in more complex steels.

Copper: improves corrosion resistance.

Manganese: improves hardenability, strength and wear resistance. It also improves the steel during the manufacturing process.

Molybdenum: improves hardenability, tensile strength and corrosion resistance (particularly pitting). It also helps to maintain the steel's strength at high temperatures.

Nickel: improves toughness, hardenability and possibly corrosion resistance.

Nitrogen: improves corrosion resistance when used in place of carbon. Nitrogen can function in a similar manner to carbon but offers unusual advantages in corrosion resistance.

Phosphorus: generally considered an impurity in blades, but improves strength, machinability and hardness for applications other than blades, but creates brittleness in high concentrations.

Silicon: improves strength. Like manganese, it makes the steel more sound during the manufacturing process.

Sulfur: generally considered an impurity in blades, but improves machinability when added in minute quantities for applications other than blades.

Tungsten: improves wear resistance. It is a carbide former. When combined properly with chromium or molybdenum, tungsten will make the steel become a high-speed steel.

Vanadium: improves wear resistance and hardenability by promoting a fine grain structure, which improves toughness and allows the blade to take a very sharp edge. It is a carbide former. Vandium carbides are the hardest carbides.

Other Common Blade Steels

1045, 1050, 1055, 1060, 1084, 1095: From 1045 up to 1095 there is an increase in carbon content. The higher the number, the more wear resistant, but the less tough (more brittle) the steel is. 1050 and 1060 are often used for swords. 1095 is the most popular of the 10 series steels for making knives. When properly heat treated, it is a reasonably tough steel, holds an edge well and it is easy to sharpen. It does, however, rust easily. It is a simple steel, which contains only carbon and manganese.

5160: A very popular steel within the bladesmithing community. Essentially a spring steel, it is very forgiving in terms of heat range for both forging and quenching. 5160 steel has great toughness and moderate edge holding ability, and is commonly used for high impact blades like swords and chopping blades.

52100 (SUJ2): This steel was developed for the ball bearing industry but has found a loyal following in the bladesmith community. Similar to 5160 but with a higher carbon content (1.0 percent vs. 0.6 percent), when expertly heat treated, it holds a better edge but is not as tough. When water quenched, performs similarly to Hitachi white steel #2.

W1, W2: Simple water hardening steels with carbon content around 1.0 percent

O1: An oil hardening steel that is also forgiving in terms of heat range for both forging and quenching. At 0.9 percent carbon, it makes good knives and is between 5160 and 52100 in toughness.

Forge Welding

Successful forge welding begins with proper mental preparation. Taking time to oil the power hammer and sweeping the floor helps me get into the right frame of mind for the task ahead.

Forge welding is one of the most difficult bladesmithing techniques to master. The theory is simple: heat two metals hot enough so that they just start to "sweat," or melt, on the outside surface only. The two pieces are placed on top of one another and struck with a hammer. The extra kinetic energy from the blow further heats up the mating surfaces and the molecules from each surface mix with each other, thus permanently joining, or welding them.

In reality, several factors complicate the process. First, when steel is heated to a high temperature and exposed to even minute amounts of oxygen, a black flake-like substance called scale forms on the outside of the steel. This scale effectively acts like a shield, barring molecules from each piece of heated metal from mixing. Secondly, differing metals have differing melting temperatures, resulting in very narrow windows of temperatures where welding of differing metals can be successfully accomplished. Thirdly, with carbon steel, there is a fine line between heating it to a welding temperature and burning it. Steel is like an apple pie insomuch as once it is burned, it is no good and must be thrown away. Also, the size of the billets must match the size of the fire in the forge that will bring steel up to welding temperature, a function of the size of the tuyere. Lastly, the size of the billet must be perfectly matched to the speed and size of the hammer blows. When the billet is ready for forge welding and removed from the fire, it immediately starts to cool down, thus making it impossible to forge weld a large billet with small slow hammer blows.

The bladesmith employs several techniques to aid in perfect forge welding. To combat the negative effects of scale, a high quality flux is

FIG. 1: A bar of Hitachi steel is heated in the forge and forged into a small core. A piece, determined by the size of the final blade, is cut off. FIG. 2: A bar of gokunantetsu is heated and split almost in two with a hot chisel under the power hammer. FIG. 3: The void resulting from splitting the steel. FIG. 4: The Hitachi steel core is inserted in the void. FIG. 5: The billet is hammered together to mate the surfaces to be welded. FIG. 6: Powder flux is sprinkled on the billet to aid in welding. FIG. 7: The billet is carefully heated up in the forge. FIG. 8: After the flux begins to bubble on the heating billet, but before the steel starts to spark, it is carefully forge welded with a precise sequence of light hammer blows. FIG. 9: The most exciting event in the bladesmithing shop: forge welding.

FIG. 1

FIG. 2

FIG. 3

FIG. 4

FIG. 5

FIG. 6

FIG. 7

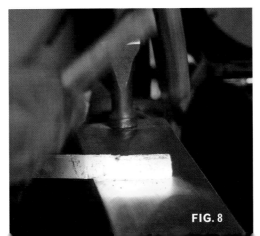

FIG. 8

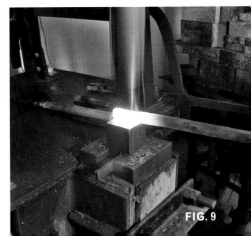

FIG. 9

Flux powder for forge welding, consisting of borax, boric acid and iron filings.

sprinkled on the billet, or between the surfaces to be welded, when the metal is about half way to forge welding temperature. This flux usually consists of borax, boric acid and iron filings, all in powder form. As the metals heat up, the flux melts like honey and covers all exposed metal to give it a protective covering from oxygen. It is also acid-like at high temperatures, dissolving any scale that may have formed prior to the application of the flux. When the pieces are hammered together, the flux is squeezed out from the void, allowing the molten molecules of iron or steel to weld.

Heating the pieces to be welded slowly, thoroughly and evenly is also important for successful forge welding. Forge welding carbon steel is usually accomplished at a yellow heat. Mating the surfaces to be welded will improve the rate of success. Slightly "doming" the surfaces before fluxing is another technique that allows the billet to weld from the inside-out, and gives the flux an easy way out. Placing the billet in the right spot in the forge fire and not disturbing it more than necessary is also important. This is easier to do in a gas forge than in a coke forge because the smith can actually see the billet in the fire during the whole heating cycle. The smith using the coke or charcoal forge has to rely on experience and subtle hints to perfect the timing.

Rehearsing the sequence of hammer blows is mandatory, or else the smith will have to make decisions about where to strike the billet after he has pulled it from the fire and when time is of the essence. The billet starts to cool down the instant it is removed from the fire and there is no time for anything other than hammer blows. Thus the expression, "Strike while the iron is hot."

Nothing will teach proper forge welding as much as repetition, thus spending a whole week repeating the same forge welding procedure is the best way to guarantee eventual success. Be prepared to burn up a whole lot of fuel, steel and exposed skin on the road to Damascus! (Anything can happen on the way to Damascus, just ask Paul!)

Nine Layer Damascus Steel Billet Composition, Prior to First Forge Weld

Gokunantetsu mild steel

Carbon steel

Surfaces slightly domed for best forge welding

An ambitious bladesmith, ready for work.

A hot coke-fueled fire, ready for work.

Forge basics

Steel must be heated more than 700 degrees Celsius before it will be pliable enough to 'work' with the bladesmith's hammer. There are several different ways to accomplish this: a coal forge, a coke forge, a charcoal forge, a gas forge or an electric forge. Each fuel or energy source has advantages and disadvantages. We will examine them in detail.

A unique feature of steel that is hotter than 700 degrees Celsius (a red heat) is that it acts like a sponge, absorbing gases and chemicals from its environment, and giving up carbon in exchange.

Starting The Forge At Carter Cutlery

FROM LEFT TO RIGHT –
FIG.1: Kindling is chopped with a freshly sharpened axe. This is the time to start focusing the mind on the work ahead. FIG. 2: The fire is laid with care, alternating paper and fine kindling. Coke will be added later. FIG. 3: The fuel is started with a match, and after the wood is burning well the air blower is plugged in. FIG. 4: Add a couple of scoops of coke and adjust the fire if necessary. A word of caution: If you disturb the fire too much before the coke catches on fire, it might go out. FIG. 5: If the blower is doing its job, you will be able to get the fire hot enough to catch the coke on fire. The flames will reduce in size when you are burning pure coke or charcoal.

FIG. 1

FIG. 2

Top to Bottom: Coal, coke and charcoal

Coal

A coal forge was the most common forge up until about the 1960s. All around the world, village blacksmiths were equipping nations with metalwork made in coal forges. Older generations will have strong memories of approaching a blacksmith's shop and smelling the distinct scent of burning coal. The unique smell is a result of the high amounts of pollutants, such as phosphorus and especially sulfur, in the fuel. These turn to gas at high heat and mix with the smoke turning it yellow.

Coal was the cheapest and most available fuel. With a coal fire, it is easy to isolate heat to any pre-determined part of the work piece (i.e., the blade) because of the design of the forge. It is perfectly adequate for most forging operations, but not very good for forging blades because of the high risk of pollutant contamination to the steel. At high temperatures, phosphorus and sulfur are absorbed by the steel, and carbon is lost in the process. The only acceptable way to use coal is to turn it into coke first. Coal is tricky to light on fire, takes some time to get up to full temperature, and comes down in temperature slowly even if the forced air supply is cut off.

Coke

A coke forge is fueled by coke, which is coal that has been heated high enough to drive off the harmful pollutant gases. It is reasonably available, inexpensive, burns very hot and clean and also has the advantage of being able to localize heat in the work piece. Occasionally there are trace amounts of sulfur and phosphorus still left in coke that was not heated high enough, so it is advisable to add coke to the burning fire when the work piece is absent. If the fire is hot enough, any residual gases will burn off within a minute or two.

Periodic maintenance is required of a coke forge by adding more coke every half-hour or so and cleaning out the "clinkers" from the bottom of the fire every couple hours. Clinkers are non-combustible impurities in the coke that melt like molten glass and conglomerate near the hottest part of the forge, the tuyere, which is also where the forced air is fed to

FIG. 3   FIG. 4   FIG. 5

Forge Diagram

Three Areas of the Fire

1. OXIDIZING LAYER
2. NEUTRAL LAYER
3. CARBURIZING LAYER

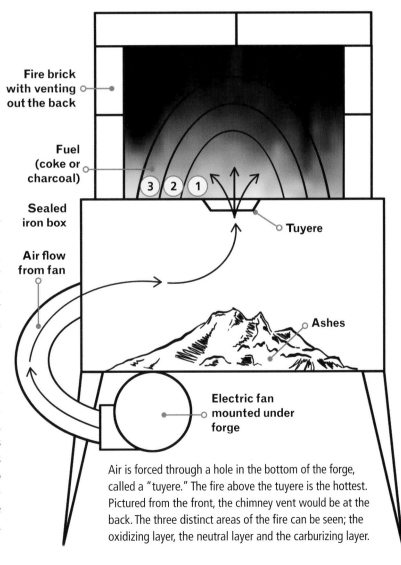

Fire brick with venting out the back

Fuel (coke or charcoal)

Sealed iron box

Air flow from fan

Tuyere

Ashes

Electric fan mounted under forge

Air is forced through a hole in the bottom of the forge, called a "tuyere." The fire above the tuyere is the hottest. Pictured from the front, the chimney vent would be at the back. The three distinct areas of the fire can be seen; the oxidizing layer, the neutral layer and the carburizing layer.

the forge. If these clinkers are not periodically removed, they will eventually cut off the air flow through the tuyere to the fire. The timing will depend on how hot the fire is and how much air flow is supplied to the forge. Coke is also difficult to light on fire, and is slow to come up to full temperature and slow to cool down.

Charcoal

A charcoal forge is fueled by charcoal, which is usually make from wood, but theoretically could be made from any organic material. Like the process of making coke from coal, charcoal is made by heating wood hot enough to drive away everything except the carbon. This has to be done in the absence of oxygen or the wood will catch on fire and burn to ashes.

A charcoal fire burns the cleanest, and the carbon rich environment is very beneficial to carbon steel. Unlike coal and coke fires, charcoal is very easy to light, and most importantly, reacts immediately to forced air input. The temperature literally 'jumps' with a blast of air, and drops suddenly with no forced air. This feature is desirable when ultimate temperature control is needed, as in the even heating of a thin blade.

Charcoal burns up more quickly than coke, and so more of it must be added between each forging operation. Because it burns so cleanly and completely, clinkers rarely form in a charcoal fire. It is also the most costly, and not commonly used outside of Japanese swordsmiths and discerning bladesmiths.

Above: Clinkers, the left over impurities from burnt coke. If the bladesmith does not remove clinkers in a timely manner, they will congeal over the tuyere and snuff out the fire.

Below: Apprentices break up large chunks of pine charcoal from Japan into smaller pieces for the forge.

There are three distinct areas of the burning fire: an oxidizing area, a neutral area and a carburizing area. In general, we want to heat blade steel in the neutral part of the flame. If the steel is sticking down into the flame, the blade will lose carbon due to an excess amount of oxygen present. It is also easy to overheat and/or burn the steel because this is the hottest part of the fire and is usually out of sight of the bladesmith. If the smith

wants to increase the amount of carbon in the steel, then heating the steel in the upper atmosphere repeatedly will result in the hot steel picking up (absorbing) some carbon. (*See pg. 43, Forge Diagram*)

Gas

A gas forge uses liquid fuel that is atomized and forced into the forge where it is combusted. Advantages include a constant fuel supply and no periodic maintenance, such as the removal of clinkers. It is also the easiest of forges to control the final temperature inside the forge. If the temperature is set low, you can heat a bar of steel while sipping a coffee and not be in fear of overheating or burning the steel. Disadvantages include noise, not being able to localize heat in only one part of the steel (basically all or nothing), and the high probability of an oxidizing atmosphere. They are very common in North America because of their simplicity of operation.

Notice the flame of a gas forge circles around the forge like a vortex.

Electricity

Electricity can be used at least two different ways to heat steel for forging. The most common way is to heat the steel in a temperature-controlled kiln or oven. This is generally the slowest method, and unless the oxygen is purged (removed) from inside the kiln, oxidation occurs. A faster way is to insert the steel inside a special wire coil, through which extremely high electrical current is passed. The resistance in the steel makes it red hot in literally seconds. If the current is strong enough, the inserted steel can even melt. Because oxidation is a factor of temperature and time, the speed of this system minimizes oxidation. This second system requires very expensive machinery and is not very common.

Forging at Carter Cutlery

Because Carter Cutlery uses coke and charcoal exclusively for all forging and heat-treating operations, forge maintenance means that the forge has to be periodically cleaned of clinkers. It must be periodically replenished with fuel, which must be built up constantly in a mound, and the steel has to be heated in the upper two-thirds (neutral or carburizing atmospheres) of the fire.

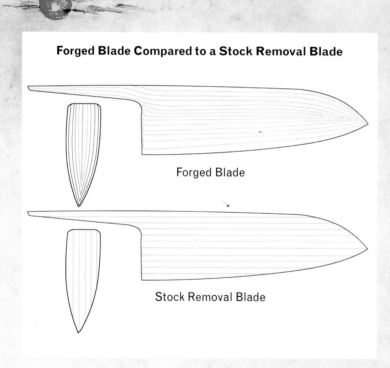

Forged Blade Compared to a Stock Removal Blade

Forged Blade

Stock Removal Blade

Forged blade compared to a stock removal blade. The grain in the steel is compressed in the forged blade, leaving close to 100 percent of original strength. The grain in the stock removal blade is ground away, weakening the blade.

Forged crane hook retains 100 percent strength of the steel. Stock removal (machined) crane hook would be weakest right where the weight is to be suspended.

Why forge to final thickness?

There is an old saying among metalsmiths that goes, "Five minutes of forging beats thirty minutes of grinding." The closer we can forge a blade to its final dimensions, the easier and faster it is to complete.

Besides the time saving advantages of forging a blade, there is also an added benefit of strengthening it. Each piece of steel has what we call "grain." The grain in steel is similar to growth rings in a tree. Even if we forge steel thinner than its original stock thickness, by packing and condensing the grain, we preserve a lot of it's inherent strength. If we were to simply grind away steel from the original piece of stock, the blade would only be as strong as the grain that remained in the blade.

I find that an example that is easy to understand is a crane hook. Crane hooks must be extremely strong to hold enormous weight. All crane hooks are forged, otherwise they would break where the grain of steel is weakest.

How to forge

This is a topic that is much easier to learn from a demonstration. However, these are some general guidelines to commit to memory.

First, you have to ascertain that the forge fire is clean, topped off with fuel and burning hot. Second, you have to have an exact idea of what shape you are trying to forge. A scaled drawing or a template of some durable (hopefully non-combustible) material should be at hand to refer to. The steel has to be heated thoroughly where you intend to manipulate it, and while you are heating it, you should be rehearsing in your head the action that you will take the instant you remove the steel from the fire. Once the steel is removed from the fire, the work needs to commence in a steady deliberate fashion, finding a rhythm that you can sustain while moving the maximum amount of metal in one heating operation, which is called "one heat." Each movement should be deliberate. Never continue to work a piece of steel if your intention has become foggy. Some metalsmiths will do a rehearsal forging out of modeling clay for projects they are attempting for the first time. This way, when they get to working hot metal, they already have a specific image in their head.

Fortunately, the blades that we forge at Carter Cutlery are not overly complex in shape or form. Although many metalsmiths forge in three planes, i.e., height, width and length, blades are mostly forged in two planes only. We hammer steel from the top, or flip it 90 degrees and hammer the sides. We almost never hammer a blade from the butt (end) or the tip (forward point). Additionally, because of the inherent qualities of the laminated steel we exclusively forge, we are mostly concerned with the final thickness of the blade. We will shear off extra material if the blade is too wide.

The most common technique used at Carter Cutlery is a clockwise forging sequence. Viewing a flat rectangular bar of evenly heated steel, we work a five inch section, starting the hammer blows along the lower left hand side of the bar, moving towards the far end of the bar, circle around to the right side of the bar, following the right side back towards the starting line, and then up the middle towards the end of the bar again. By following this pattern, the steel can "flow" from high areas to low areas, in other words, the steel will flow in the direction of least resistance. Continue this action until the bar cools to its lower forging temperature.

Above: Forging steel with a traditional Japanese Bladesmithing hammer, given to me by my teacher YoshiyukiSakemoto.

Bottom Left: Forging the curve in a kitchen knife with the power hammer.

Bottom Center: Hot-work knife used for scraping scale and other impurities off the heated steel.

Bottom Right: Be sure to clean the steel to be forged each time you pull it out of the fire to prevent large scale and bits of coke from being beaten into the surface of the knife.

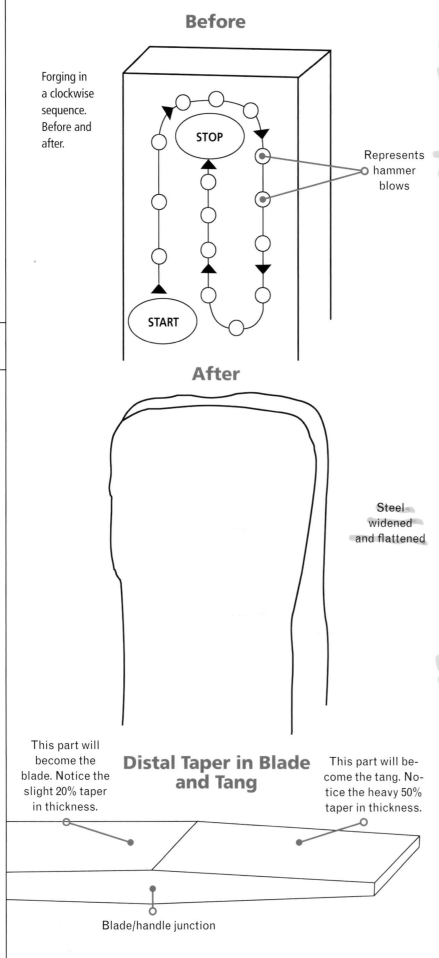

Before

Forging in a clockwise sequence. Before and after.

STOP

Represents hammer blows

START

After

Steel widened and flattened

This part will become the blade. Notice the slight 20% taper in thickness.

Distal Taper in Blade and Tang

This part will become the tang. Notice the heavy 50% taper in thickness.

Blade/handle junction

After each clockwise forging sequence, the bar has to be inspected for thickness, either by eye or with a set of calipers. Forging a length greater than five inches requires that the next forging sequence overlap the first one by a few inches to blend the work of different heats. Desirable features of forged blades are distal tapers in the blade and tang (handle portion). The blade should be thickest at the blade/handle junction, and taper roughly 20 percent towards the tip of the blade and 50 percent towards the butt of the knife.

The forging sequence for forge welding often varies from the sequence described above, the main concern being that the molten flux has a way of escaping from the surfaces to be welded.

Scale removal

If steel is heated past 650 degrees C in the presence of oxygen, scale will form on the surface. This scale should be removed from annealed blades before proceeding with further steps. There are at least four common ways to remove scale from Japanese blades; by grinding, by acid bath, by sand blasting and by hammering over a concave surface.

Grinding involves removing the top layer of affected steel through the process of abrasion. This technique wastes some material and will leave the steel thinner than its final forged dimensions. Therefore, when scale removal is to be accomplished by grinding, allowances have to be made when forging. Due to the extreme hardness of scale, it can be costly in terms of abrasives.

Annealed blades can be immersed in an acid, such as sulfuric acid, and the acid will loosen and dissolve the scale. If the strength of the acid is appropriate and the timing is right, very little other

Flakes of scale on the power hammer anvil that fall off hot steel as it is forged.

When scale removal is to be accomplished by grinding, allowances have to be made when forging.

than the scale, i.e., the steel itself, is removed. If you forget about your blades while they are soaking, you may wonder where they disappeared to when you finally remember to look for them in the acid. Using acid is always dangerous, and disposal of old acid can be problematic at best.

Carter Cutlery does not recommend the use of acid for scale removal.

Sand blasting is a very economical, expedient and safe way to remove scale from annealed blades. Only the scale is removed, leaving all of the original steel.

Some of the dust produced by a sand blasting cabinet is harmful to the lungs, so proper ventilation and respirators are necessary. Sand blasting is the preferred way to remove scale from blades at Carter Cutlery.

The traditional Japanese way to remove scale from thin cutlery is to hammer it over a concave depression in a wooden stump. As the hammer strikes and the blade bends into the depression, the scale on the reverse side flies off. Every section of both sides of the blade is worked over until the scale is removed. This technique has the additional advantage of metallurgically working the steel, a process called cold forging.

Traditional Curved Stump Technique

Above: "Ol' Dusty" is our trusty sand blast cabinet at Carter Cutlery.

Right & Opposite Page: Traditional scale removal on curved stump technique.

Cold forging

A common technique used by Japanese bladesmiths but seldom exploited by western cutlers is the process of cold forging. In simple terms, cold forging is the mechanical reduction in the steel's grain size through force when the steel is below normal forging temperatures. Cold forging

Top Left: Cold forging, starting at the lower left hand corner.

Top Center: Cold forging around clockwise.

Top Right: Cold forging up the middle.

makes the steel denser. In its extreme, cold forging is done with the steel at room temperature. Amongst metallurgists, the value of cold forging is controversial, because the theory doesn't match up with reality.

Metallurgists argue that while cold forging does work-harden steel, the effects of cold forging are nullified when the steel is later heated to the temperature required for quenching. Further, they argue, cold forging will induce micro fractures in the steel that will eventually cause a hardened blade to fail under duress. I have conducted research that supports the attributes of cold forging in blades, and all highly respected Japanese bladesmiths incorporate the process. Japanese bladesmiths unanimously agree that cold forging enhances cutting performance in blades. In the final analysis, it is difficult to argue with the results.

Here are some thoughts and considerations. Carbon/mild steel laminates seem to really benefit from cold forging and do not generally show evidence of micro cracking. While I have seen homogenous blade fracture from too much cold forging, in 16,000 blades, rarely have I seen a laminate blade fail as a result of cold forging. I suspect that the softer outer laminations absorb excess force and energy, thus protecting the inner carbon steel from over stress. On the other hand, I have purposely destroyed a laminated blade by cold forging it until the blade fractured. Therefore, the amount of cold forging is a factor that must be understood.

The generally accepted practice of cold forging involves striking the properly annealed blade with moderate hammer blows until every part of the blade has been struck once. The blade is then flipped over to the other

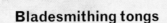

Bladesmithing tongs

It is common for a Japanese bladesmith apprentice to master several skills in the forge and around the shop before ever forging steel into blades. This was also common with western blacksmith apprentices who made nothing but hand-forged nails for years before being allowed to tackle other projects. This system not only forces the apprentice to master some basics, but also serves as a test for him to demonstrate his dedication, determination and tenacity. I know of at least one Japanese swordsmith apprentice who quit after four years of just chopping up pine charcoal. That was too bad because it is in the fifth year that the master shares his secrets with the apprentice. The mastersmith knows that if the apprentice has been diligent, he will have learned most of what he needs to know by watching master everyday at work while he was cutting the coal!

One of the skills to master as a bladesmith before making knives is making tongs of various shapes and sizes to hold hot metal. One result of my atypical apprenticeship was that I never was forced to learn how to make good tongs. I wish that I had learned this valuable skill, because good tongs can make all the difference in the world! I mention this to emphasize the importance of mastering the basic skills as well as the more interesting, complex techniques. Sometime soon I'll set aside a week of time to refine my tong-making skills.

I have purposely destroyed a laminated blade by cold forging it until the blade fractured. The amount of cold forging is a factor that must be understood.

side and the process repeated. A few more blows to straighten the blade in preparation of quenching, and cold forging is considered complete. The blades that I have experimentally destroyed required this procedure to be repeated many more times before the blades would crack. As a general rule, Yasuki white steel can withstand more cold forging than blue steel before failure.

Another benefit of cold forging is that the blows of the polished hammer and anvil face make the blade very smooth and shiny. Minor adjustments in the thickness and blade profile can be made as well. Again, in order for the student smith to appreciate the process and value of cold forging, it must be experienced first hand.

Left: Partial tang blades before (top) and after (bottom) cold forging. You can see how the blades elongated slightly from the cold forging.

Annealed blade with scale, sand blasted blade and shiny cold forged blade.

Lamination Techniques

Most western blades are made from homogeneous steel; either carbon steel or stainless steel. Advantages are simplicity of construction, low cost, lateral strength (strength from side to side) and friction co-efficient when cutting through certain mediums. Disadvantages include having to compromise between hardness and toughness, the possibility of the blade breaking in two if it is fully hardened and difficulty when sharpening both the primary and secondary edge.

Kuro-uchi kitchen knife above a stainless fukugo-zai counterpart below.

Kata-ha Blade Cross-Section Diagram

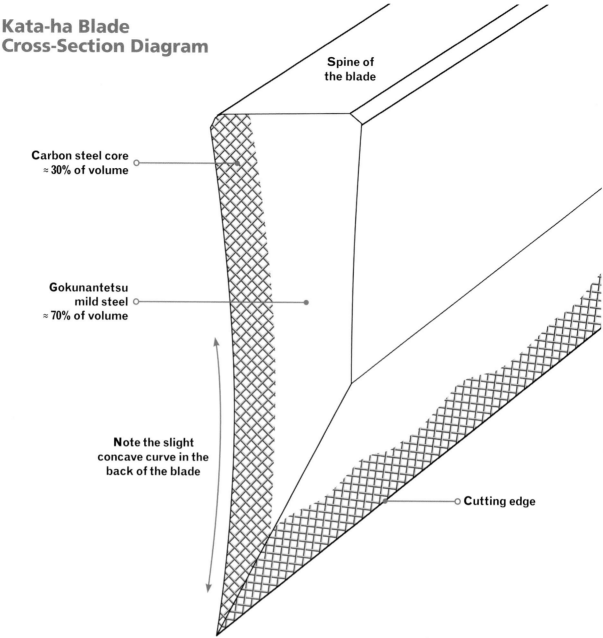

Spine of the blade

Carbon steel core
≈ 30% of volume

Gokunantetsu
mild steel
≈ 70% of volume

Note the slight
concave curve in the
back of the blade

Cutting edge

Traditional Japanese blades are made by laminating two or more steels together. In doing so, the dilemma of having to compromise hardness for toughness is alleviated. The carbon steel is fully hardened while the other softer steel acts as a toughening laminate. Laminated blades take less time to sharpen away any given amount of material. There are many ways to laminate Japanese blades. I will explain the most common techniques in detail. They are Kata-ha, San-mai, Kobuse and Damascus steel.

Kata-ha

Kata-ha laminate consists of two layers of steel, mild steel on one side and carbon steel welded to the other. The finished blade is ground and sharpened in such a way as to expose the carbon steel on the cutting edge. As a general rule, the carbon steel content is less than 30 percent of the billet.

Kata-ha laminate is used for high quality professional Japanese chef knives and for certain tools such as chisels, carpenter's plane blades and

San-mai Blade
Cross-Section Diagram

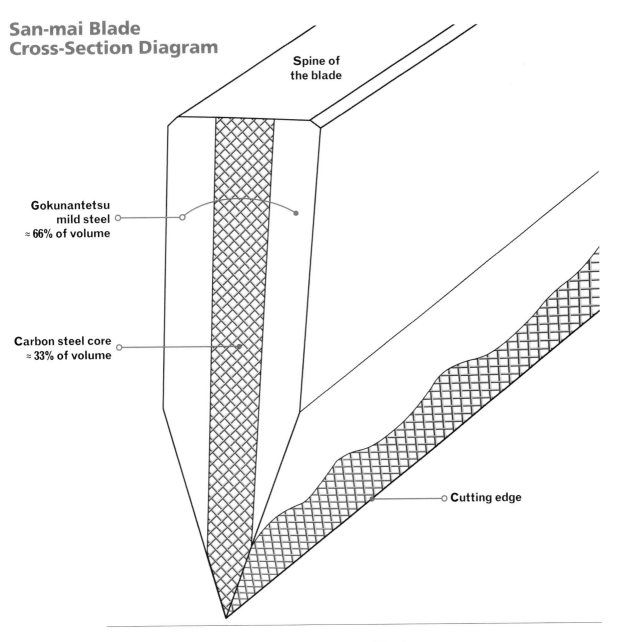

**Spine of
the blade**

**Gokunantetsu
mild steel**
≈ 66% of volume

Carbon steel core
≈ 33% of volume

Cutting edge

tree limbing koshi-nata (machetes). One needs to familiarize oneself with the use of kata-ha blades, they cut differently from most other blades. Regular maintenance, such as sharpening and straightening, presents some unique challenges as well.

San-mai

San-mai laminate is akin to an Oreo-brand cookie. The outer dark cookies are soft steel and the inner white cream is the steel core. This style of lamination is commonly found on blades that have a symmetrical grind, i.e., the edge is ground from both sides of the blade down to expose the core steel which becomes the edge. The carbon steel layer is generally a third (33 percent) of the billet. San–mai literally means "three layers." As it is a generic term, no company can trade mark or register the term.

San-mai blades traditionally use Gukunan-tetsu (clean mild steel) as the outer laminate. A modern interpretation substitutes mild steel with

Kobuse Blade Cross-Section & Blade After Repeated Sharpenings (Tsukareta)

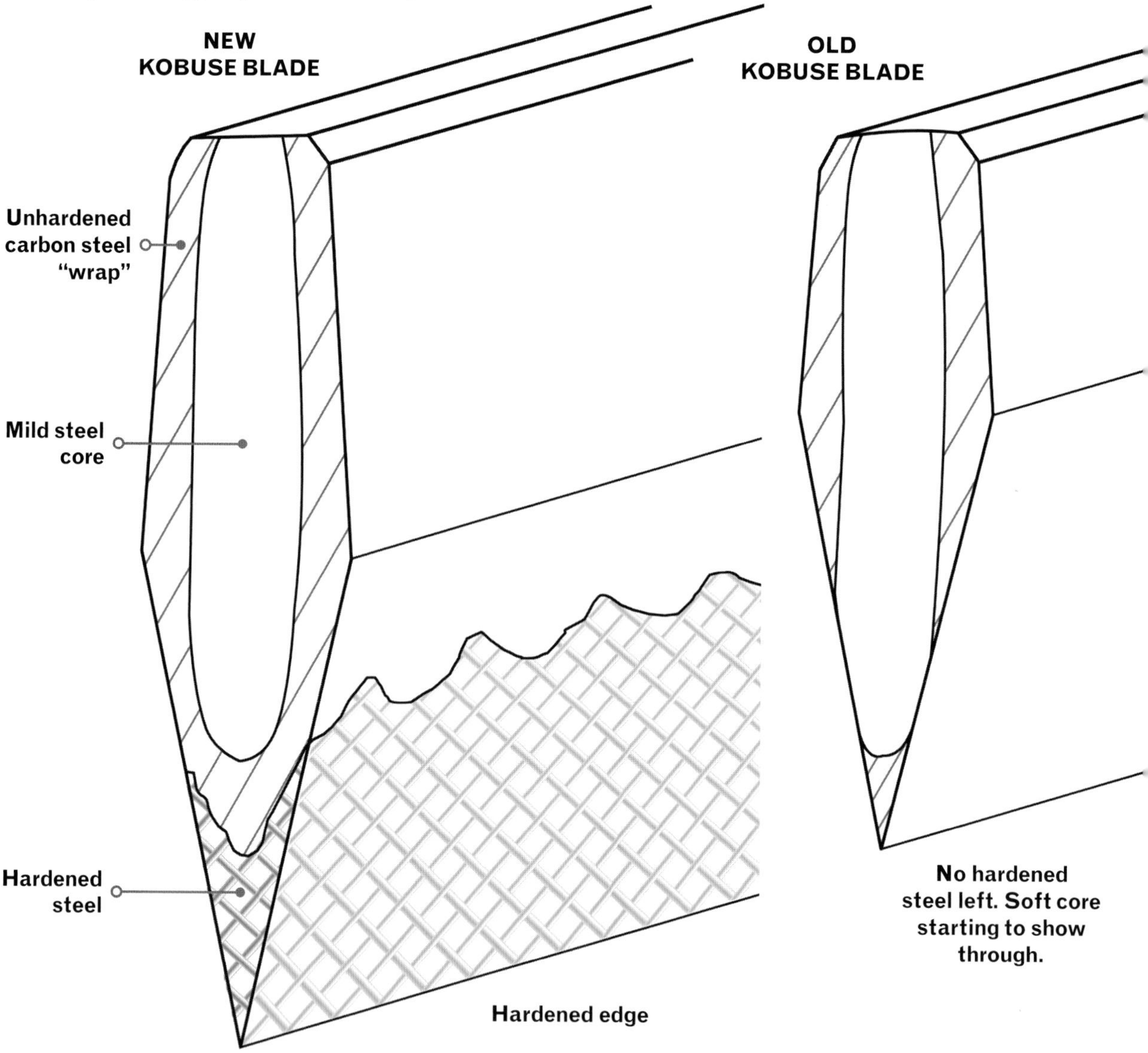

NEW KOBUSE BLADE

OLD KOBUSE BLADE

Unhardened carbon steel "wrap"

Mild steel core

Hardened steel

Hardened edge

No hardened steel left. Soft core starting to show through.

soft stainless steel, thus offering a blade which has more rust resistance. Welding stainless steel to carbon steel requires sophisticated equipment and techniques.

Kobuse

Kobuse blades are the fundamental reverse of san-mai blades. Soft steel is used for an inner "toughening" core and the outside is wrapped with carbon steel. The carbon steel is wrapped in such a way as to become the edge of the blade. This construction is most commonly found in the Samurai swords. A major disadvantage to this style of blade is that the blade is rendered useless after a predetermined number of sharpenings, as the wrapped carbon steel is completely ground away. This does not occur with a kata-ha or san-mai laminate blades, which can be used until the blade is literally sharpened away to nothing.

Damascus

Damascus laminate is made from at least two types of dissimilar steel, often with pure nickel sheet thrown in the mix for visual effect. Several layers are welded together at the same time and drawn out. The resulting mass is folded onto itself and welded again to double the layer count. This process continues until the desired layer count is achieved. Additional manipulation such as twisting, drilling, cutting and restacking can produce spectacular patterns in the finished blade. The difficulty making perfect Damascus lies in the fact that each and every forge weld must be perfect or a flaw will show in the finished blade.

Laminating at Carter Cutlery

At Carter Cutlery, we laminate our own kata-ha, carbon steel/mild steel san-mai and Damascus. The carbon steel/ stainless san-mai is purchased from a company that has multi-million dollar equipment and has been specializing in laminating this steel for decades.

Damascus steel blades made by Carter Cutlery are some of the most incredible blades in the world. They demonstrate several features that make them truly unique. The steels selected are the best money can buy. They are void of significant impurities and perfectly mixed to gain the best strength, flexibility, visual effect, ease of maintenance and superior cutting ability. The patterns chosen, namely ladder random and twist patterns, offer the best structural integrity. I expect customers to really use these Damascus steel blades. Despite hours of investment in forging a billet of Damascus steel, I anneal and then heavily cold forge each Damascus blade. Many people would shudder to think of pounding a precious Damascus blade while it is cold. On top of that, each blade is then heated in

A 17 layer damascus billet being welded in a hydraulic press. Each layer is clearly visable.

The Making of a Damascus Knife

Right: The process represented by one picture: the stacked billet, the forge welded billet of 577 layers, the heat treated blade and the final product.

FIG. 1

FIG. 2

F

FIG. 4

FIG. 5

FI

a charcoal fire and then quenched in water. If each forge weld isn't perfect, the blade could literally delaminate in the severe quenching medium of water. I don't know any other bladesmiths in the world who regularly fully quench their Damascus blades, containing carbon steel over 1.2 percent, in water.

The following is an excerpt from my first catalog:

"I normally construct my Damascus with S25C (Japanese version of 1025) low carbon steel, Gokunan-tetsu and pure nickel sheet for the outside layers and then forge weld a core of White Steel #2 in the center for optimal cutting performance. In some cases I forge weld Blue steel #2 with White steel #2 making a billet with over 200 layers and then use this material for the center core.

"In June 1999 I passed the American Bladesmith Society Mastersmith cutting performance test under the supervision of William F. Moran. The blade I tested with was of the same construction as that above, with a 200 layer Damascus steel core. Bill Moran said to me that my test blade performed better than any other he had ever seen perform the test. After cutting rope, chopping two-by-fours, shaving hair and then bending the blade to more than 90 degrees in a vise, Bill used the tested portion of my blade to shave the hairs off his forearm one more time. As he did this he whistled in amazement."

FIG. 1: Cutting gokunantetsu wafers with the hot chisel under the power hammer. Be careful not to cut all the way through, which will mar the anvil. FIG. 2: Wafers of gokunantetsu and pure nickel sheet are forged with a slight dome and cut to the same dimensions; roughly 1.25 inches by 3.5 inches by 0.25 inch. FIG. 3: All surfaces to be forge welded are ground clean. FIG. 4: The billet is stacked alternatively, steel, nickel, steel, nickel, etc. FIG. 5: The billet is held together by C clamps. FIG. 6: One end of the stack is MIG welded to keep the stack from falling apart in the forge. FIG. 7: The stacked billet is slowly heated in the forge. FIG. 8: The heated billet is carefully pried open with a work knife. FIG. 9: Each layer is sprinkled with flux. FIG. 10: The billet is closed back up.

FIG. 7

FIG. 8

FIG. 9

FIG. 10

FIG. 11: The billet is evened up on the sides. FIG. 12: The outer surfaces of the billet are fluxed some more. FIG. 13: Just after the flux starts to bubble but before the billet sparks, the billet is carefully forged from the center first, then progressively towards the outer edges of the billet. This allows the molten flux to escape. FIG. 14: This is not a time to day dream or lose your concentration. This forge welding operation is a "make it or break it" deal! FIG. 15: The high temperatures of forge welding produces a lot of forging scale, seen here surrounding the billet. FIG. 16: The forge welded billet is domed on the surface, then cut in exactly the middle, but not all the way through.

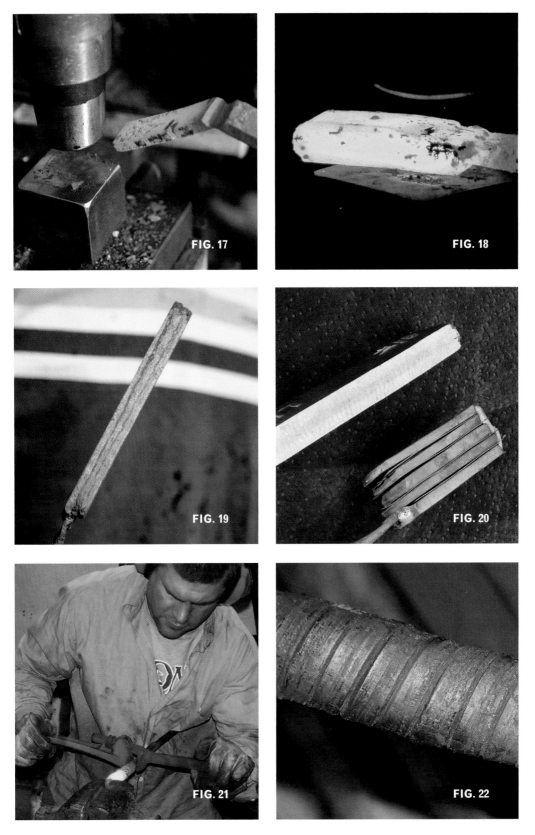

FIG. 17: The surfaces are fluxed and then folded on to one another. The welding process repeated itself. FIG. 18: When the desired layer count is half way reached, a core of Hitachi steel is inserted between the Damascus layers on the last fold, and forge welded. FIG. 19: Damascus billet complete with carbon steel center core. FIG. 20: From start to finish, several hours and several forge welding operations. FIG. 21: Before the carbon steel core is added, damascus steel can be twisted for visual effect and integrity. FIG. 22: Close up of twisted damascus steel before it is forge welded to a steel core.

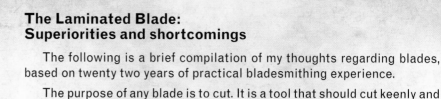

The Laminated Blade:
Superiorities and shortcomings

The following is a brief compilation of my thoughts regarding blades, based on twenty two years of practical bladesmithing experience.

The purpose of any blade is to cut. It is a tool that should cut keenly and consistently over a reasonable length of time. It is this practical cutting requirement that has led metallurgists to proclaim the superiority of carbon steel above all else as a cutting metal. This is supported by the fact that it is truly rare to find a professional in any tool-using environment who does not use a form of carbon steel for this purpose.

When worked appropriately, heat treated correctly, and given proper edge geometry, high quality cutlery grade carbon steel produces a combination of edge keenness, edge retention, flexibility, and ease of sharpening that is unparalleled by any other material.

I am often disappointed by the commercially available blades that I periodically examine. It seems to me that the blade industry has shifted the emphasis from products featuring true cutting ability to products that are strong and tough. These products will cut adequately for a brief period of time, but are well below the potential of cutting performance offered by modern metallurgical technology.

I will take the liberty of defining toughness and strength in order to clarify my point. I define toughness as the ability of a steel to resist breaking. Strength I define as the capacity of a steel to sustain the application of force without yielding its structural integrity.

For example, a lead pipe can be abused extensively, it will deform, but it is difficult to chip or crack. The lead pipe illustrates my concept of tough. Strength may be illustrated by clamping a piece of metal in a vise, and attempting to bend it. It's sustained unwillingness to yield and bend is strength.

Modern marketing trends and techinques have led people to believe that a blade's value lies in its strength rather than its traditional function, which is to retain a keen edge over a practical period of usage and be easy to resharpen.

The result of this is that we have a plethora of commercially available butterknives that may also be utilized as mini-crowbars, but a dearth of practical cutting instruments.

Within a piece of cutlery-grade carbon steel, there is a complex relationship between enduring keenness, toughness and strength. This relationship depends upon the hardness of the steel after heat treating. In the cutlery industry, hardness is measured by utilizing a point system which starts at 20 points and increases incrementally until it reaches 80 points. This is known as the Rockwell "C" scale, commonly represented by the abbreviation Rc. In general, the higher the Rc rating, the keener the steel is when sharpened. The lower the Rc rating, the tougher the steel is.

Steel is generally considered strong when it takes much force to bend it, and then springs back to its original dimensions. The problem with this situation is that the steel has been heat-treated like a spring (Rc 55) rather than a blade designed for cutting.

In my opinion, a steel blade heat-treated to Rc 63-64 would produce amazing keenness with enough toughness and strength to withstand repeated use. However, at this hardness, the slightest abuse would probably result in a broken blade. Personally, I believe that blades should not be made to withstand abuse, to the detriment of their cutting ability. Enter the laminated blade.

With laminated blades, there doesn't have to be a trade-off between edge hardness, keenness and toughness. By utilizing a high carbon (over one percent carbon) cutlery steel core laminated between two layers of lower carbon steel, one can maintain an edge hardness of Rc 63 to 64 while achieving any level of toughness or strength desired via the choice of outer laminations.

For example, wrought iron laminated to a center core of cutlery steel will give the ultimate combination of toughness and hardness. 1035 steel laminated to a center core of cutlery steel will give a blade spring like qualities without compromising edge hardness.

In addition, stainless steels may be used as the outer laminate, almost eliminating the historical drawback of carbon steel: rust.

However, not all available laminations fully utilize this potential advantage. For example, some commercially available three-layer blades utilize a combination of an AUS 8 stainless steel core enveloped by two slabs of 420J2 stainless steel. There are two problems inherent in this combination;

- Commercially tempered AUS 8 stainless steel merely attains an Rc 59 approximate hardness. This is not nearly enough to achieve excellent edge retention and keenness.

- Commercially tempered 420J2 stainless steel reaches Rc 53 approximate hardness. This is, for all intents and purposes, way too hard to qualify as a "toughening" laminate.

I have seen similar blades snap cleanly in half under minor stresses.

At Carter Cutlery we produce eight lines of hand forged cutlery: our traditional line of Japanese two-layer and three-layer hand-forged kitchen cutlery, and custom knives that blend the best of hand-forging and material technology.

Homogenous steel blades make for striking comparisons. For example, a "normal" homogenous steel blade will cut through a fresh piece of bamboo twenty times. When slapped forcefully against the same bamboo it will either break or remain perfectly straight (depending on it's composition and manufacturing processes).

One of my typical three layer laminated blades will cut the same bamboo two hundred times. When slapped forcefully against the bamboo it will bend somewhat, but not break. It can then be easily restraightened to cut the bamboo another two hundred times. This is a knife, not a crowbar!

Heat Treating

Blades anneal (slowly cool) in a bucket of rice straw ashes

Traditional annealing techniques

Annealing is the first operation of the thermal cycle of heat treating, and occurs prior to quenching and tempering. When steel is heated in the forge and then worked, a certain amount of molecular stress builds up in the steel as the grain is pushed this way and that. Annealing the steel involves heating it thoroughly to the predetermined temperature and then covering the steel in an insulating cover so that it can cool very slowly. The heating and then slow cooling allows the molecules in the steel to rearrange in the most stable formation possible, thus removing the stress. Steel should reach its maximum ductility (softness, as opposed to hardness) after proper annealing.

Technically, there are three processes related to annealing; full annealing, process annealing and normalizing. Full annealing is a time consuming process that is done inside a computer controlled kiln, where the steel temperature is brought down a given amount over a given time, for example, starting at 750 degrees Celsius, dropping the temperature 30 degrees every 30 minutes until room temperature. Normalizing involves heating the steel thoroughly until the proper annealing temperature is reached, removing from the fire and then setting the steel aside to air cool.

At Carter Cutlery we use process annealing. Japanese blades actually benefit from a bit of calculated stress inside the steel. It contributes to their overall cutting performance, therefore it is not beneficial to fully anneal. In the chapter on cold forging, I will explain what positive attributes stress can have on a high quality blade. The insulating material we use for annealing at Carter Cutlery is a bucket of rice-straw ashes.

Each year in Japan, after the season's rice is harvested, the bladesmith acquires several truckloads of rice straw. Once it has dried sufficiently, the bladesmith burns the straw in such a way as to recover all the ashes. The ashes are put into a five-gallon bucket, tamping them down as they are inserted. Amazingly, the ashes of several truckloads of straw will fit in the bucket. With use, the ashes will turn to a very fine powder, and each year it is necessary to add more fresh ashes.

Blades that have been forged to their final dimensions are heated in the forge to the proper annealing temperature, held at that temperature until the steel is heated thoroughly, and then inserted hastily into the bucket of straw ashes tip first, until the whole blade is covered. The blade is not disturbed until the temperature has dropped below 250 degrees Celsius, (480 degrees Fahrenheit). In practice, it is common to anneal blades last thing before closing up the shop for the day. That way they can be left until the next morning.

The blades that were left to cool in the bucket of rice straw ashes are carefully removed so as to minimize wastage of the ashes. Some ashes will be stuck to the blades. The blades are brushed off with a soft brass wire brush allowing the ashes to fall back into the bucket. A bucket of very fine powder ashes represents a huge investment in time and energy, and the fine ashes are irreplaceable except by the passage of time. No kidding, if my shop catches on fire, I'm going back in for my bucket of ashes!

Heated blade being inserted into the bucket of rice straw ashes to anneal.

The bladesmith must know what the proper annealing temperature looks and feels like. After annealing hundreds (thousands?) of blades, the timing and temperature will feel "just right" when it is just right.

Temperature control in annealing

The challenge for the bladesmith is not only to commit to memory the proper annealing temperature, but also to know what that temperature looks and feels like. I can tell you that Hitachi white steel at 760 degrees looks bright red, slightly orange, but until the student smith sees the teacher anneal several blades, it will be difficult to visually read the temperatures. As for the importance of feeling the steel, of course I don't mean that you have to touch red hot steel to test it! Rather, I am talking about the more subtle aspect of how the bar or steel vibrates as it heats up in the fire. The molecular changes that occur inside the steel give off tiny vibrations. I am also talking about the intangible ability of intuition. After annealing hundreds (thousands?) of blades, the timing and temperature will feel "just right" when it is just right. Again, knowledge of the theory isn't comparable to the benefit of experience.

Something else to consider is how ambient light affects the look of hot steel. Steel that is 650 degrees C will appear red when removed from the fire and viewed in darkness. The same piece of steel held up to the bright sunny sky will look black. Watch out, many serious burns in the bladesmith shop are from steel that didn't look hot! Similarly, steel just a few degrees shy of melting will look like it's at normal forging temperature in the sunlight. The fastest way to burn up steel is to try forge welding outdoors on a sunny day. Please don't ask me why I know that. Even during daylight, the ambient light is very different on a rainy day as it is on a clear day.

At Carter Cutlery we try take as many of the variables out of the lighting as possible. When annealing and quenching, we close the doors and windows and cover them, and turn on a little 40-watt lamp behind us, several feet from the fire. The result is that the conditions for reading the temperature of the steel are favorable and consistent.

Stamping the maker's mark &DRILLING

If you wish to stamp your blades with a touchmark, now is the time to do it, before the blade is hardened through the process of quenching. Even though a laminate blade might "take" the touchmark after quenching, there is a risk of damaging the blade. A homogeneous blade will damage the touchmark if stamping it is attempted after the quenching procedure.

Sometimes deep stamping of a maker's mark will distort the steel around the stamp mark. Check profiles and adjust if necessary before quenching. Double check for straightness and twisting as well.

Quenching

Quenching, the second operation of the thermal cycle of heat treating, is the process of thoroughly

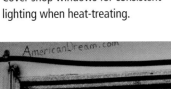

Cover shop windows for consistent lighting when heat-treating.

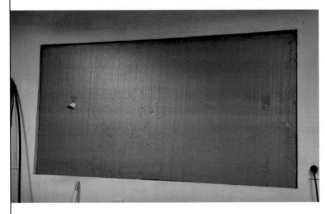

heating a blade to its proper quenching temperature and then quickly freezing all molecular activity inside the steel by cooling it rapidly. How hot the steel must be heated will depend on the nature and chemical composition of the steel. The rate at which the steel must be cooled will depend on the same factors.

The goal of quenching is to harden the steel so the blade will cut well and hold a good edge. Remember that the carbon content of the steel will determine how hard the blade will get after quenching at the proper temperature. Likewise, the carbon content will also determine how fast the blade must be cooled in order for the blade to reach its maximum hardness potential. As a general rule, the higher the carbon content, the

Stamp the blade with the maker's mark on the anvil. Make sure the anvil is clean, or you will end up with dents on the reverse side of the blade.

Various stamps are used at Carter Cutlery.

The heated blade is rapidly cooled by plunging into quenchant.

more precise the heating operation required and the faster the blade must be cooled.

The objective in quenching the blade at the proper temperature is to achieve the optimal grain structure inside the steel. Optimal grain structure is defined as the smallest grain size possible, and at the same time, having reached it's full hardening potential. For each different type of carbon steel, this happens at a very specific temperature, called the critical temperature. Heating above the critical temperature and quenching will result in a blade that has fully hardened, but with larger than optimal grain size. The higher the heat, the larger the grain size. The goal is to quench steel at the lowest possible temperature and yet have the blade fully harden.

Quenching actually consists of two operations: thorough heating and quenching.

Heating a blade in preparation for quenching

In theory, heating a blade for quenching is the same as heating during forging or for annealing. In practice, it is by far the most difficult to heat a blade properly for quenching. There are two reasons for this. First, the blade for quenching has to be evenly heated throughout the whole blade, with no discrepancy in visible color or feel. Second, that evenly heated blade has to be EXACTLY the correct temperature, i.e., the critical temperature, as well. It is easy to heat a short square bar of steel evenly, but extremely difficult to heat a long, wide, thin blade evenly. There is a real tendency to get nervous knowing that you are about to give birth to

Prepare a hot charcoal fire for heating to quench.

Only the utmost focused attention will ensure superior quenched knives. Mentally ready yourself for the critical job ahead.

the blade! There is no turning back once the blade is removed from the forge and quenched in the coolant. You will either have a perfectly hardened blade, or you will not.

There are some techniques the Japanese bladesmith uses to aid in thorough and even heating of a blade for quenching. The forge is preheated so that heat reflects off the inside walls of the forge. A nice clean fire of pine charcoal is built up, and a steady medium blast of air is fed to the fire. The blade to be heated, having been straightened, stamped and drilled if necessary, is cleaned of any oil or grease. It is then coated in a very thin layer of akatsuchi doro (red clay mud). The muddied blade is dried over the fire, and left above the fire to preheat. The blade is then thrust into the fire, carefully containing the charcoal with the forge poker on the back end of the fire so that the inserted blade doesn't push half the pile to the back of the forge. The goal is to heat the thickest parts of the blade first and then 'bleed' the heat into the thinner, more delicate parts of the blade.

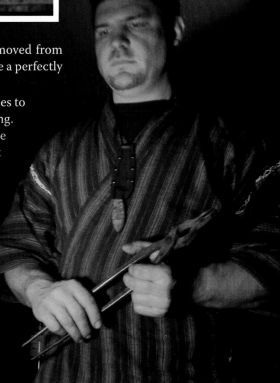

FIG.1: Blade must be free from oil and grease. FIG. 2: The blade is coated in akatsuchi doro - red clay mud. FIG. 3: The clay must have just the perfect viscosity. FIG. 4: Wet clay on the top blade compared to dry clay on the bottom. The dry clay is thin enough to read newsprint through.

FIG. 1

FIG. 2

The blade can never remain still when heating, rather, it must stay in constant motion. When the blade is pulled through the fire towards the smith, the charcoal must again be contained with the poker so that charcoal doesn't spill out of the forge. The smith must constantly 'fuss' with the coal, as the blade is being pushed forwards and pulled backwards, so that the charcoal remains in a nice pile over the tuyere. As soon as the blade starts to turn a dull red color, the medium force blast of air is reduced to a light blast. The blade is kept in constant motion until the heat from the glowing coals brings the blade to the correct temperature. There is no way around it, this is an intense experience. With repetition, heating for quenching becomes a little easier, but it still remains an intense experience.

"Doro nuri san nen": Coating clay, three years

As easy as the task may seem, traditional Japanese bladesmiths attach tremendous importance to the skill of properly coating blades in clay for quenching. Thus the common saying "Doro nuri san nen." It takes three years of study before the apprentice is considered ready to coat blades in clay professionally. One challenge is to add the right amount of water to the clay to make a slurry with the proper viscosity.

Also, applying the right amount of clay to the blade in all the right places and drying the clay on the blade requires acquired skill and discipline. Not just any old clay will do, either! Each bladesmith secures his clay secretly, and adds all sorts of concoctions to give him the competitive advantage.

The clay has to expand with the blade as it is being heated in the fire. It has to be hard enough to not flake off while being heated, and it shouldn't crack either. When the clay is coated thinly on the blade, the clay layer prevents bubbles from forming next to the cooling steel as it is thrust into the quenching water. The blade cools faster this way. When applied thickly to the spine of a blade, as in sword quenching, the clay prevents water from coming in contact with the steel that must stay soft.

FIG. 3

FIG. 4

Quenching the heated blade

The heated blade is then quickly plunged into a waiting bucket of coolant, the blade perpendicular with the surface of the coolant. This is most commonly done in oil or water for most blades of carbon steel. Oil is a medium speed quenching medium, suitable for blades that have a carbon content between 0.5 percent and 1.0 percent. These blades will have a cooling time between one and two seconds. We use the term 'gentle' to describe an oil quench, because blades are not prone to twisting or warping in oil compared to a water quench.

Water is a quicker quenching medium. It is suitable for blades with a carbon content over 1.1 percent. Remember that Yasuki white and blue steel are over 1.2 percent carbon. These blades must cool in less than one second to fully harden. Water, unfortunately, is a 'severe' quenching medium, and bending and twisting are not uncommon for water quenched blades. However, if a blade of more than 1.1 percent carbon content is quenched in oil, it is not likely to fully harden.

REBAR

Bars of mild steel are heated in the forge in preparation for quenching, then used to heat the quenching water prior to quenching blades. Temperature of the water should be about 28 degrees Celsius.

When using oil or water for quenching, it is common to increase the viscosity by preheating. Viscosity means the fluidity of the liquid and affects the ability to cool down steel. As a general rule, oil reaches its maximum viscosity at 80 degrees C, 176 Fahrenheit, and water at 28 degrees C, 82 Fahrenheit. Each individual smith will have a 'secret' temperature that they feel is best for their blades.

This brings us to the purpose of coating the blades in akatsuchi doro before heating them for quenching. The akatsuchi prevents the formation of bubbles that occur when a hot blade is plunged into water. If bubbles were to form, they would insulate the steel from being cooled immediately. The application of akatsuchi is the 'secret' that enables Japanese bladesmiths to fully harden blades made from Yasuki steel.

The blade is removed from the water before it fully cools to the temperature of the water. In theory, the blade needs to cool quickly from its critical temperature to 250 degrees C, 482 Fahrenheit, and then slowly from 250 to room temperature. That means that the blade has to be removed from the quenching bucket before the blade reaches the temperature of the coolant. Watching a Japanese master smith is the best way to get a feel for this.

Finally, the blade is tested for hardness. A file can be used to test for hardness by seeing if the teeth will "bite" into the hardened steel. A more common way in Japan is to see if the hardened blade will shave steel filings from some permanent object in the shop. My band saw table has a very visible, and growing gouge where each blade is tested before it gets the approval for further completion. Quenching is followed by tempering.

Tempering

Tempering, the third operation of the thermal cycle of heat treating, is the process of reheating a quenched and fully hardened blade to a given

Below Left: In a darkened room, a heated blade is quenched in a bucket of luke-warm water.

Below Right: Steam rises from the quenched steel.

Left: A properly quenched blade shaves filings from the band saw table.

Below: Small filings being cut from the corner of the band saw table indicate a successful quench.

temperature to remove some of the brittleness and to make the blade useful. Tempering is done at a much lower temperature than annealing or quenching. An analogy is a rubber balloon. Annealing steel can be compared to an empty flaccid balloon. Quenching the steel is like a balloon so full that it almost bursts. Tempering would be like letting a little bit of air out of the balloon so that it is resilient to light impact. Tempering results in an inflated balloon that is tough and useful.

Because of the relatively low temperatures involved, tempering can be accomplished in as many ways as a creative person could imagine, as long as the blade is heated to the correct temperature and held there for more than several minutes. I have tried tempering:

- over a fire,
- on the hot bricks of the burning forge,
- in an electric kiln,
- in a hot oil fryer,
- on an electric stove coil,
- with a gas torch,
- in an oven, and
- on a hot copper block.

In all of the above methods, the trick is to know what the temperature is at any given moment. In the case of the kiln, oil fryer and oven, you can set the thermostat to the desired setting. This will work as long as the thermostat reading is accurate. It usually isn't. Therefore it is necessary to check the posted temperatures against a reliable independent thermometer. Better yet, learn some visual aids to read the steel's temperature. I'll discuss the most common methods of visual confirmation of tempering temperatures and share the Japanese secret method as well.

Tempering by color

The most common way to visually read tempering temperatures in steel is by watching for color changes as it heats. For most carbon steels, the tempering range is between 160-250 degrees C. The steel must be ground and somewhat polished for this to work. The steel must also be free from oils and other contaminants. As steel is heated slowly, it will start to oxi-

Below: Tempering over a fire.
Right: Tempering on the hot bricks of the burning forge.

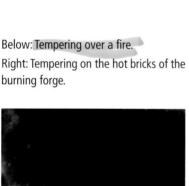

FIG. 1 Tempering with a gas torch.
FIG. 2 Tempering in an electric kiln.
FIG. 3 Tempering in a hot oil fryer.
FIG. 4 Tempering on an electric stove coil.
FIG. 5 Tempering in an oven.

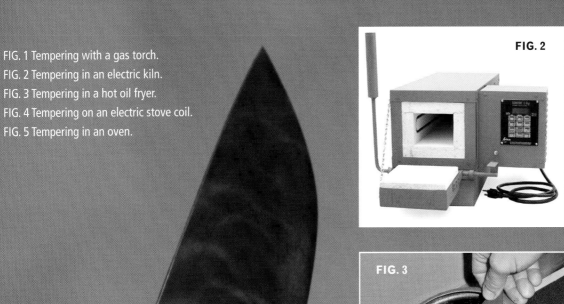

FIG. 2

FIG. 3

FIG. 4

FIG. 5

FIG. 1

The color range of polished carbon steel.

dize, and change first from shiny metal to pale yellow, to bright yellow, straw yellow, brown, purple, dark blue and then light blue.

Each color represents a given temperature for a given steel. For high performance blades, we rarely temper beyond straw yellow. If the blade turns purple or blue at any time (including the grinding operations later) the temper will be ruined. Blades tempered using the oxidizing colors as a guide will usually need to be cooled in water when the desired color is obtained, or else heat in the blade will continue the process beyond what is desirable.

Tempering using Tempilstik® temperature indicators

Tempil, Inc., of South Plainfield, NJ, markets a special product called Tempilstik, which is sold through the retailer Centaur Forge (see appendix). The Tempilstik is the size and shape of a pen, with a special chalk core and an aluminum outer shell. The chalk core is exposed from the tip and applied to a blade as one would mark with a piece of chalk. When the blade is heated to a predetermined temperature, the chalk melts, indicating that its temperature has been reached. There are close to 100 different Tempilstiks available, all indicating different temperatures. The one closest to the technical tempering

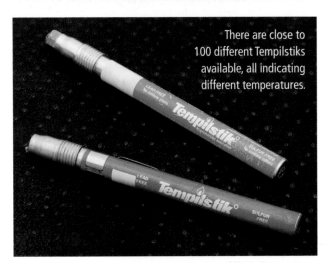

There are close to 100 different Tempilstiks available, all indicating different temperatures.

When the blade is heated to a predetermined temperature, the chalk melts, indicating that its temperature has been reached.

temperature is selected, applied to the blade, and the blade heated until the chalk melts. The blade is then removed from the heat source.

At Carter Cutlery, we commonly temper our blades on the hot bricks of the forge and employ a Tempilstik to monitor tempering. A word of caution: The melted chalk indicates that the desired temperature has been reached, but not how much hotter the blade got. Be sure to remove the blades as soon as the chalk melts.

Japanese water drop tempering method relies on the behavior of drops of water on the hot blade.

Tempering by the Japanese Water Drop method

Tempering using the ancient Japanese bladesmith method is accurate and convenient because it is not necessary to first grind and polish the blade. The quenched blade is slowly heated over the fire and periodically the smith checks the heat in the blade by dipping his hand into the quenching bucket and then flicking it with drops of water. The behavior of the water drops on the hot blade indicates the temperature.

The relationship of water drops on the hot steel are as follows:

- Water falls on blade, slowly evaporates 60-80 degrees C.
- Water immediately evaporates 80-100 degrees C.
- Water spreads and then bubbles/evaporates 100-120 degrees C.
- Water marks blade then hisses for half second 120-140 degrees C.
- Water doesn't mark blade, hisses for less than a quarter second 140-160 degrees C.
- Water dances on blade, evaporates 160-180 degrees C.
- Water bounces off of blade 180-200+ degrees C.

Blades that will be subject to stress and shock, such as a machete or cleaver, should be tempered multiple times.

Straightening

While most people assume that handheld blades are perfectly straight, the sad reality is that most blades are not straight. In fact, not only are most blades bent, but many are twisted as well. Now, my definition of a straight blade is not theoretical, but practical. A theoretically straight blade would resemble a laser beam. Such a blade would be an anomaly. Practically speaking, a straight blade is a blade that is not perceptibly bent one way or another upon proper examination by the trained and experienced human eye. Such a blade is desirable, because only when a blade is straight and untwisted can the maximum performance be wrung from it.

Knife blades are only designed to be strong in two directions; from the tip to the hilt, and from the edge up to the spine. If the blade is twisted, it will fail when force is applied directly into the tip.

So why are so many blades far from being straight? The answer lies in the fact that most people, knifemakers included, have not been taught to carefully examine blades. There are five steps to examining blades for straightness and twisting. Having the proper light for blade examination is extremely important. Indoor electrical lights are poor because they cast shadows and obscure the blade's true features. I recommend an outdoor blade-examining station where blades can be examined against the backdrop of the sky. Overcast days are preferable to bright sunny days. A blade must be clean to examine it properly.

Directions of strength in a blade.

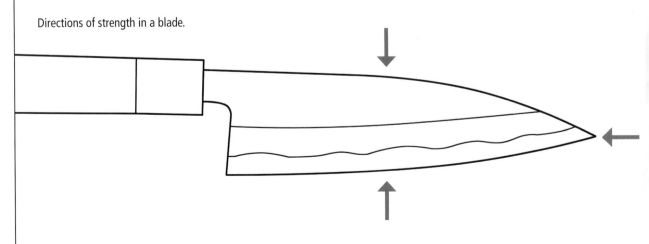

Five steps of blade straightness diagnosis (BSD)

To diagnose the straightness of a blade, the first step is to hold the blade in such a way that the handle is furthest away from you, with the edge of the knife towards the ground and the point aimed at your dominant eye. The non-dominant eye is closed. The back, or spine, of the knife should be in full view. Not only can the spine be examined for straightness this way, but straightness from the blade continuing to the end of the handle can be examined. Some blades are reasonably straight, only to cant off significantly from the start of the handle. Almost all blades will be bent one way or the other.

The second step is to re-examine the blade in the same manner, this time with the edge of the blade up.

Far left: Outdoor straightening station.
Above: Knife pointed at eye, edge down.

Below left: Blade pointed at eye, edge up.
Below middle & right: Blade edge towards eye, horizontal, blade tip towards support side.

The third step is to hold the handle of the blade in the dominant hand and point the tip of the blade towards the support-hand side with the edge of the blade pointed straight towards the eyes. Close the non dominant eye. Now you can examine for twisting. Compared to the heel of the blade, the tip of the blade may be twisted down or up, called a simple twist. The twisting may be more severe, in that it twists different directions in more than one place. This is called a complex twist.

The fourth step is to hold the handle in your dominant hand, handle away from you and the tip of the blade pointing at your dominant eye, as in steps one and two, but with the flat of the blade horizontal. Position yourself so that natural light reflects off the surface of the blade. This examination will confirm what you detected in steps one, two and three.

The fifth step is to repeat step four but flipping the blade over 180 degrees so that the edge is pointed the opposite direction.

Correcting bent blades

There are five common ways to fix a bent blade. The appropriate method will depend on the steel in the blade, the hardness and or brittleness of the blade and the extent of the bend. These techniques are:

1. Hammer with brass hammer on wooden stump.
2. Straighten with magebo.
3. Straighten in a vise.
4. Press in vise between three pieces of wood dowel.
5. Use tagane.

Straightening bent blades involves using tremendous force, which in some circumstances can cause a blade to snap. Safety goggles are recommended for all straightening procedures.

Hammering with brass hammer on a wooden stump

Slight bends in a blade (less than 20 degrees) can be forcefully hammered out if the blade has not been quenched (homogenous) or if the blade is a carbon steel/mild steel laminate. A brass hammer and a wooden stump are used to minimize the shock to the blade. Using the first and second steps of blade straightness diagnosis (BSD), the portion of the blade that is

Blade horizontal, flat side up, pointed at eye.

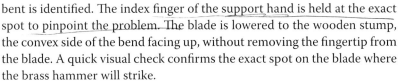

bent is identified. The index finger of the support hand is held at the exact spot to pinpoint the problem. The blade is lowered to the wooden stump, the convex side of the bend facing up, without removing the fingertip from the blade. A quick visual check confirms the exact spot on the blade where the brass hammer will strike.

As the dominant hand reaches for the hammer, the support hand breaks contact with the blade in order to hold the blade by the handle in preparation for the coming hammer blow. One very light strike to confirm accuracy of the technique is followed by a more forceful blow. The blade is reexamined for results, and repeated if necessary. In this technique the emphasis is on proper diagnosis rather than on hammering technique.

At Carter Cutlery, due to the inherent properties of the laminated blades we make, hammering with the brass hammer and straightening with a magebo are generally used for straightening.

Straightening with magebo (Japanese blade bending stick)

Left: Pinpoint the problem area with the finger tip.
Top right: Place the blade on stump/anvil.
Bottom right: Hammer as necessary to correct the bend.

To straighten a blade with the magebo, the blade is placed in the notch of the stick and torqued straight.

Above: Straightening a blade in a vise takes more time than the hammer and magebo methods.

Above middle & right: Pressing the blade in a vise with dowels is a very precise technique.

In this technique, the magebo straightening stick (from Japanese "mage(ru)," to bend, and "bo" meaning stick) takes the place of the hammer. The bend is located using BSD steps one and two and then the blade is placed in the notch of the stick and torqued straight. This technique is less stressful to the steel than hammering. The blade is reexamined and the process repeated if necessary.

Straightening in a vise

Straightening the blade in a vise differs from the magebo in that the portion of the blade that is held in the vise is immobile and remains unbending. Thus the force of the effort to straighten is concentrated into a smaller area. Inserting the blade to exactly the correct place is the key to this technique. Compared to the first and second techniques, straightening with the vise takes more time.

Pressing in a vise between three pieces of wooden dowels

If the bend is in a hardened homogenous blade, the most controlled way to apply force to straighten it, and thus the most gentle, is to use the three-dowel-in-the-vise technique. Two wooden dowels are taped to the inside of one of the vise jaws, the dowels straight up and down to the vise. A third dowel is taped to the opposite vise jaw, positioned between the first two dowels. The bent blade is inserted between all the dowels, the bent area in contact with the single dowel. The vise is closed slowly, until the bend is straightened. This is a very precise technique, but also the most time consuming.

Using tagane (a cold chisel)

Using a tagane to straighten blades is a secret technique "borrowed" from the hand-forged saw masters. It is used for hardened blades that refuse to be straightened by any of the above techniques. The bent blade is placed on a steel anvil, the concave side of the bend facing up. The tagane, which is a small carbide chisel-shaped tip brazed onto a hammer-like tool, is struck multiple times, actually penetrating the surface of the steel. This causes the steel to the sides of the cut to be displaced out from the cut, thus expanding that area of the blade. The direction of the cuts caused by the tagane will affect the direction of expansion. The tagane is used until the blade reaches the desired straightness. Following this severe process, the blade must be ground to remove the many unsightly tagane chisel marks. The blade often partially returns to its original state with grinding, so it is often necessary to expand the blade past the point of being straight, so that when the blade is ground and polished, it will return to a point of perfection.

It is difficult to calculate just how much tagane persuasion a bent blade may require, and so this is more an art than a science. In Japan, straightening with the tagane is considered a full time profession, and the art is in danger of being lost because of a lack of interest from the younger generation.

The tagane tool is used for hardened blades that refuse to be straightened by any of the above techniques.

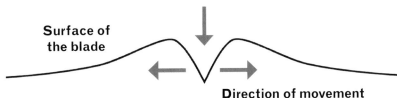

Groove from tagane hammer blow

Surface of the blade

Direction of movement

Above: Metal displaced by the tagane, blade moves outward from tagane hammer blow.

Correcting twisted blades

Using step three from BSD, the tip of the blade may appear twisted up compared to the heel of the blade, or it may appear twisted down. This will indicate a simple twist. If the blade first twisted up and then down, or visa versa, the blade has a complex twist. Straightening twisted blades can be accomplished by hammering with brass hammer on wooden stump, straightening in a vise or using the tagane.

If the blade has a tip that is twisted up, when held in the dominant hand with the tip facing away from you, then the rule to go by is the blade will be hammered from the lower dominant side tang/ blade junction, up towards the tip on the other side of the blade,. If the tip is twisted down, then the blade is hammered down, starting on the dominant hand side near the tip of the blade, down towards the handle on the support hand side.

Imagine a rectangular blade. The four corners are labeled A,B,C and D. Starting at The tang/blade junction moving clockwise, we will call the corner on the support side A, the corner on the support side tip B, the dominant hand side tip C and the dominant hand side blade/tang junction D. When the blade tip is twisted up upon examination, lay the blade on the stump with the tip away from you, and hammer up from D to B. The blade can be flipped over and hammered again in the same direction. If the blade tip is twisted down, hammer down from C to A. Flip and repeat if necessary. Simply stated; twist is up, hammer up. Twist is down, hammer down, always starting from the dominant hand side.

Straightening in a vise

For thick blades that are twisted, it may be necessary to untwist them in the vise. A hineribo, a special un-twisting tool (from "hineru," to twist, and "bo," a stick) is needed, similar to the magebo, but made for twist-

Illustration of rectangle with corners A,B,C and D

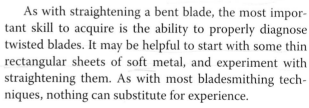

Untwist a blade using a vise and a hineribo.

Series above: Hammering "up" a blade to fix a twist that is "up" for a right handed person. Series below: Hammering "down" a blade to fix a twist that is "down" for a right handed person.

ing and not bending. A pair of adjustable pliers or adjustable wrench can by employed in a pinch. The handle is secured in the vise and the blade is torqued with the hineribo the opposite direction of the twist. The blade is examined and corrected as necessary.

Using tagane

A twisted blade can be straightened by the careful use of the tagane. The chisel edge of the tagane must be struck parallel to the direction of the twist, thus expanding the metal and forcing out the twist.

Proper diagnosis is critical

As with straightening a bent blade, the most important skill to acquire is the ability to properly diagnose twisted blades. It may be helpful to start with some thin rectangular sheets of soft metal, and experiment with straightening them. As with most bladesmithing techniques, nothing can substitute for experience.

WARNING: It is not uncommon to experience extreme eye fatigue from looking closely at blades for too long. When this happens, stop and move on to a different activity, and don't return to blade straightening for at least an hour or so.

Grinding A Perfect Blade Profile

Now that the blade is forged, annealed, free from scale, cold forged and straightened, the shape of the blade, or profile, must be precisely ground. Grinding is the operation of using files or other abrasives to mechanically shape the steel into a functional blade. Grinding can be divided into two categories: grinding the blade profile and grinding the blade's edges (secondary and primary). We'll cover the edges in a later chapter. For now, let's talk about the profile.

At this stage, the template is scribed onto the billet of steel that will become your knife. Place the pattern so that it most appropriately covers the billet in relation to the thickness and tang.

Below: Metal shears are bolted down to the concrete floor for stability. Bottom Left: Shear in motion. The top blade is manually operated via a long lever. Bottom Middle: Sheared sliver is still attached to the blade. Bottom Right: Cutting excess material with steel shears is the fastest way to get close to the desired final dimensions of a blade. This freshly cut out blade is held next to the pattern for comparison.

Grinding a forged blade's profile can be done with a variety of tools. Heating the blade via friction is not a big concern because this grinding is done prior to heat-treating (annealing, quenching and tempering). As you read in the chapter on forging, the blade needs to be shaped after a pattern or template. At this stage that template is scribed onto the billet of steel that is to become your knife. Place the pattern so that it most appropriately covers the billet in relation to the thickness and tang.

Be careful on full tang knife billets to orient the template the correct way. I once made the mistake of switching the tang end of the billet for the blade end and ended up with a blade with way too much taper. Once the template is in place, secure it with a pair of locking pliers or strong clamps. Any sharp-pointed tool that is harder than the annealed steel will scribe (scratch) lines on to the billet. Trace around the template completely. Examine it before you remove the clamp(s) to make sure you can see the scribe lines clearly.

Examine it again, checking it against this list:
- Are the lines clear and not making little train tracks?
- Is the blade/tang junction exactly where it should be?
- Is the blade where it should be?

If you have made a mistake scribing the lines, you can lightly grind the surface and scribe again, but you will now be committed to grinding and polishing the flats of your finished blade. Also remember that, on a laminated billet, if you grind steel from one side you really ought to grind the same amount from the other side as well, or the steel core will no longer line up in the middle. For blades that are meant to have a forge finish or a hammer forge finish, these options will no longer be possible, so take great care when scribing lines on a billet.

There are several methods for removing the excess steel from the billet to produce the perfect profile. We'll examine each one:

- Steel shears
- Cut-off wheel
- Band saw
- Drill press and hack saw
- Belt sander
- Bench grinder
- Kaiten toishi

In Japan it is common to spot what looks like a giant pair of scissors that the smith uses to snip off extra metal as he forges out the bil- lets for blades. When the steel is at forging temperature, steel up to 10mm thick of can be sheared. Cutting excess material in this way is simply the fastest way to get close to the desired final dimensions of a blade. However, it is limited to straight or slightly curved cuts. Cold forging later will make it necessary to remove some metal down to the final profile. These shears are a major time saving device to the Japanese bladesmith.

Lacking metal shears, the next fastest way to remove excess steel from a blade billet (also referred to as "cutting the blade out") is with a circular abrasive cut-off wheel. Rather than use the abrasive wheel in the conventional manner by securing the workpiece in the adjustable clamps and lowering the rotating wheel straight down to cut it, we hold the workpiece (the billet) in our (gloved) hands and push into the moving blade. Little chunks of steel are removed at a time, and in the matter of a few minutes a 300mm blade can be cut out.

The process sounds more dangerous than it really is, but certain precautions must be taken to avoid an uncomfortable injury. Care must be taken to not cut into or beyond the scribed lines. With practice, this method is another great time saver, and the thin blade is even able to cut small radii and sharp corners. It can be used with great precision. Gloves, a mask and full eye protection are mandatory with this machine.

A band saw with a metal cutting blade can be used in the same way

Above Right: The abrasive cut-off wheel is another quick way to remove excess steel from the blade billet. Above Left: Rather than use the abrasive wheel in the conventional manner, hold the workpiece (the billet) in your gloved hands and push into the moving blade.

Below: Cut out the blade profile with a metal-cutting saw blade in the band saw.

Use the small wheel attachment to precisely grind semi-circular finger grooves.

With a fresh #36 or #40 grit belt, a belt grinder can be used at the highest speed to grind away excess metal. Be sure to buy one with a variable speed control.

as cutting wood on the band saw. Care must be taken to not cut into or beyond the scribed lines. Limitations include not being able to cut tight radii and the cost of band saw blades. Beware of finger positioning in relation to the moving blade and be sure to use a push stick to feed the workpiece into the blade.

In a small shop void of any of the above tools, it is possible to cut out the blade from a billet with a drill press and a hand-powered metal-cutting hack saw. Start by drilling as many holes as possible around the scribe lines. Be careful to not drill over the scribed lines. Once holes have been drilled all around the perimeter of the blade, carefully place the billet in a bench vise and cut out with a hack saw, cutting from hole to hole. Make a sheath of thick leather to hold the billet in the vise to avoid scratching the metal. Once the blade is cut out completely, a hand file can be used to complete the shaping process. This process is the most time consuming.

If the smith has a 2x72-inch belt sander, a fresh #36 or #40 grit belt can be used at the highest speed to grind all the excess metal away. Be careful of heat buildup, frequently cooling the billet in water. This method creates a lot of dust and sparks. It is a common method among western knifemakers. Gloves, a mask and full eye protection are mandatory with this machine.

A bench grinder can be used similarly to the belt sander. Gloves, a mask and full eye protection are mandatory with this machine.

While not primarily used to do heavy profiling of blades, the rotating water stones are more than capable of grinding steel off of places you don't want it. I often use it for minor adjustments as I also grind the secondary and primary edges of heat treated blades.

Kaiten toishi rotating water stones

The Kaiten toishi is one of the amazing tools that allows Japanese bladesmiths to put out the incredible production capacity for which they are known. Fast, accurate, cost effective and simple are words that best describe this tool. However, what is not readily apparent to the observer is that 90 percent of using the Kaiten toishi effectively is proper upkeep and dressing of the stones. It takes the diligent student at least 5000 ground blades before he will fully comprehend the intricacies of maintaining this great machine.

Above Left: Profiling a blade with the bench grinder is a good option when the amount of steel to take off is minimal. Note, a dust mask should be worn for this machine.

Above Right: Note how fingers and hands stay well away from the powerful grinding wheel. Make sure there is minimal gap between the platen and the wheel, lest your fingers get caught and pulled down through.

Right: The Kaiten toishi can be used to grind slight adjustments to the profile.

Below Left: Ninety percent of using the Kaiten toishi effectively is proper upkeep and dressing of the stones.

Below Right: (Top) Mark the stone in motion with a crayon to identify the high spots. Below Right: (Bottom) The high spots on the stone are evident as red spots once the stone has been turned off and stops spinning.

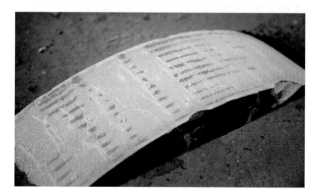

Left: It takes the diligent student at least 5000 ground blades to fully comprehend the intricacies of maintaining this great machine.
Above: Dress the stone with the toishi tagane.

Another difficulty the aspiring bladesmith will face is the lack of availability of these fine wheels anywhere outside of Japan. If the student takes the time to find a good stone and then is determined to learn its use, he will be rewarded beyond his expectations for his perseverance.

Tips to achieve the perfect profile

As the smith is cutting out or grinding the blade profile, the scribed lines, which should be clearly visible, are the guide. As soon as you are so close to the lines that you are actually touching them in places, it is necessary to employ another "micro observation" technique to be in full control of the profile. In a good source of natural light, hold the blade at eye height with the flats of the blade horizontal. Instead of focusing your attention on the flats, look closely at the outer edges of the blade. If you hold the blade with the point towards your eye, the spine of the blade should look compressed into a few millimeters. Compressed like this, every high or low spot on your scribed line will be evident. Similarly, every line on the outer profile of the blade should be examined this way. In the pattern or template you used, every line should be well defined and with a purpose. Ask yourself if the lines you are now looking at were meant to be perfectly straight, curved or pointed.

Pinpoint trouble areas, then attempt to grind in a way to affect only those areas and re-examine. At this stage, the blade should be at 97 percent of its final profile. The other three percent will be removed in the final polishing stages.

To evaluate the blade profile, hold the blade at eye height with the flats of the blade horizontal.

Drilling Holes

To attach handles to a full tang knife securely, we will need two types of holes drilled through the tang: pin holes and bridge holes.

Pin holes

Full tang knives that are to have a handle attached for completion will need some holes drilled through their tangs. Through these holes will go pins that will mechanically keep the handles from falling off in the event that the epoxy bond fails. These holes are accomplished with a drill press. Any artistic arrangement or size of holes can be chosen for the pins, but at Carter Cutlery we generally utilize three pins, one near the handle/blade junction, one near the end of the handle, and one in the center, spaced evenly between the two.

Before holes can be drilled, it is necessary to mark them by tapping a center punch with a hammer on the exact spot to be drilled. This leaves an indent and makes drilling more precise. The two holes near the ends of the handle can be 'guestimated' by sight, but the middle hole must be measured.

With a set of protractors or calipers, mark equidistant lines from the first two holes to find dead center. The third hole should be marked with the center punch just slightly forward of center, perhaps by a hair or two. This will give the finished knife a balanced look. If the center pin is slightly toward the rear pin, the knife will look rear-end heavy.

Before the holes are drilled, examine the blade according to the fourth step of blade straighness diagnosis: Hold the blade in your dominant hand, handle away from you, with the tip of the knife pointed at your dominant eye and the flat of the blade parallel to the ground. The three center

The tang of this Whitecrane knife includes both small pin holes and large bridge holes.

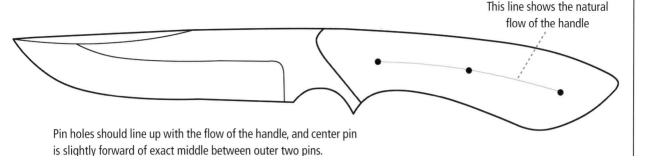

This line shows the natural flow of the handle

Pin holes should line up with the flow of the handle, and center pin is slightly forward of exact middle between outer two pins.

punch marks should follow the shape of the handle, and not be in visual conflict. If the handle curves down from the blade/ handle junction, then the pin holes should also form a curve down. If the handle has some upswing, as in a Japanese sword, the pin holes should mirror that upswing.

If the marked holes pass visual inspection, commence drilling with the appropriate size drill bit. At Carter Cutlery, we prefer not to use any oil when drilling. If the drill bit can't drill the steel easily, we stop and sharpen the bit. Occasionally, a blue super steel tang needs to be annealed a second time before drilling.

Once the pin holes have been drilled, remove the drill bit from the drill press and insert a drill bit much larger than the first. With this drill bit, chamfer the edges of the three holes just drilled.

Above: Use the drill press to drill holes in the tang and to chamfer the holes.

Bridge holes

Using the same drill bit used to chamfer the pin holes, drill several holes between the pin holes, preferably two bridge holes between each pin hole. These holes will allow epoxy to flow from one side of the blade tang to the other, making a cement bridge between the handle material. It is a much stronger bond than just gluing the handle material to the metal tang alone.

The trick is to not drill any bridge holes that will structurally weaken the tang. A rule of thumb is to never drill closer to the edge of the profile than twice the steel thickness. For example, if you were drilling bridge holes in a tang that was 2mm thick, you wouldn't want to drill any closer than 4mm from the edge. This guideline is also how you determine the appropriate size drill bit for bridge holes.

Once the bridge holes are drilled, the edges are once again chamfered with a larger drill bit.

Grinding the Secondary and Primary Edges

Secondary & Primary Edges

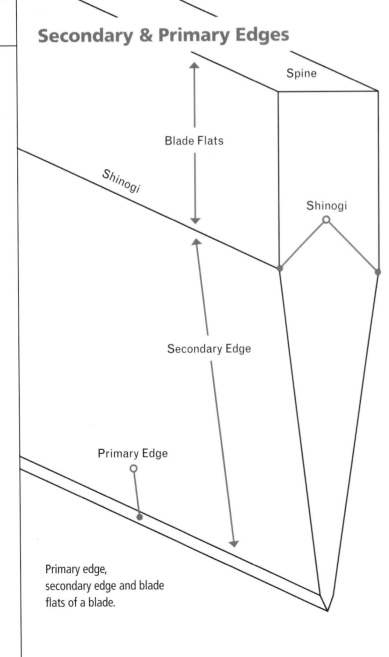

Primary edge, secondary edge and blade flats of a blade.

Grinding is the process of using files or other abrasives to mechanically shape the steel into a functional blade. Grinding can be divided into two categories: grinding the blade profile and grinding the blade's edges (secondary and primary). Grinding a forged blade's profile is usually done with a variety of bench grinders. Heating the blade via friction is not a big concern because this grinding is done prior to heat-treating (annealing, quenching and tempering). When grinding the secondary and primary edges after heat treating however, it is critical not to heat the blade above 180 degrees Celcius at any time. This is one of the bladesmithing operations that brings to light a sharp contrast between western and Japanese blade making philosophies and practices. (See the essay "Philosophy of Japanese Metallurgy" later in this chapter.)

Of all the metals used by man, carbon steel is one of the most difficult to shape through grinding; this is the reason for forging to final dimensions whenever possible. Complicating matters is the fact that hardened carbon steel is many times more difficult to grind than annealed steel. For this reason, western blademaking places an emphasis on grinding the blade as much as possible before heat treating. On the other hand, Japanese bladesmithing is characterized by grinding the blade profile only, and then heat-treating the blade before establishing the secondary edges via grinding.

Leaving the edge thick ensures that the steel will harden evenly throughout the blade. On the other hand, if the edge was ground thin and the spine of the blade thick, the thin steel would cool quicker than the thick steel and the hardness would also vary, i.e., harder on the edge and softer towards the spine. From the Japanese perspective, this variance in hardness is not desirable. As the blade is sharpened repeatedly over the years, the blade owner would experience a drop in cutting performance, as the edge worked its way up into softer steel.

The 'secret weapon' that Japanese bladesmiths use that allows for efficient grinding of fully hardened steel is the Kaiten toishi, or water-cooled rotating grinding stone. These stones rotate in a trough of water, which allows for very quick removal of metal without the danger of affecting the blade's temper. The greatest difficulty in using Kaiten toishi is the maintenance of the stones themselves. If regular maintenance is not properly conducted, the stones will wear unevenly and become out of true roundness. When the stones are well cared for, one can grind with amazing precision considering how large the stones are. There are several types of stones, some being natural quarried stones and others synthetic. Of the synthetic stones, concrete-based and epoxy-based are the most common. The stones are fairly expensive, and the machine they run on usually has to be fabricated by the bladesmith himself or contracted to a steel welder.

Below Left: Kaiten toishi water stones.

Below Right: Spray containing steel and stone particles from thousands of ground knives builds up on the splash board over the years of use.

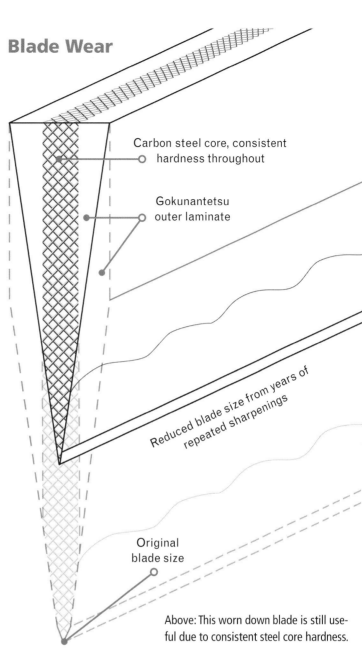

Blade Wear

Carbon steel core, consistent hardness throughout

Gokunantetsu outer laminate

Reduced blade size from years of repeated sharpenings

Original blade size

Above: This worn down blade is still useful due to consistent steel core hardness.

Above: Two different grit Kaiten toishi are used by bladesmiths.

Below: All grinders at Carter Cutlery, except the bench grinder, rotate up and away from the worker.

Two different Kaiten toishi are used by most Japanese bladesmiths, the difference being grit size and revolutions per minute (speed). The first stone is usually under 100 grit abrasive and spins at roughly 400 rpm. The second 'finishing' stone is usually close to 400 grit and spins a bit slower. The stones are wired electrically so that the motion of direction is away from the bladesmith. These stones set the pattern, as the smith will try to arrange all rotating wheels in the shop to rotate in the same fashion. The exception is the bench grinder, which needs to rotate towards the bladesmith due to the nature of its use.

One of the tricks to ensure even and controlled grinding is to quickly establish a bevel on the blade, and to let the rotating stone find the same bevel each time the blade is held against the stone. This is a skill that must be acquired through experience. Because the smith cannot see the contact between the stone and the blade, he must develop a feel for this operation. Every few seconds the blade is removed from the rotating stones and inspected. Grind lines can be adjusted as necessary by changing the pressure position on the blade. The amount of grinding is determined by the design of the blade. If the blade is not straight, it will be evident during grinding. It is almost always necessary to adjust straightness during grinding.

Secondary edges ground in a blade on the Kaiten toishi can be concave, flat or convex. Constant grinding without any forward/ backwards movement in the blade will result in a concave or 'hollow' grind. A flat grind can be accomplished by a slight backwards and forwards rocking motion in the wrists as the blade contacts the stone. A concave edge is accomplished by a more pronounced rocking motion. As with all grinding operations, the blade is examined every few seconds and adjustments to the motions are made as necessary. To polish a secondary edge after it has been established using the Kaiten toishi, a very slow moving belt sander can be used.

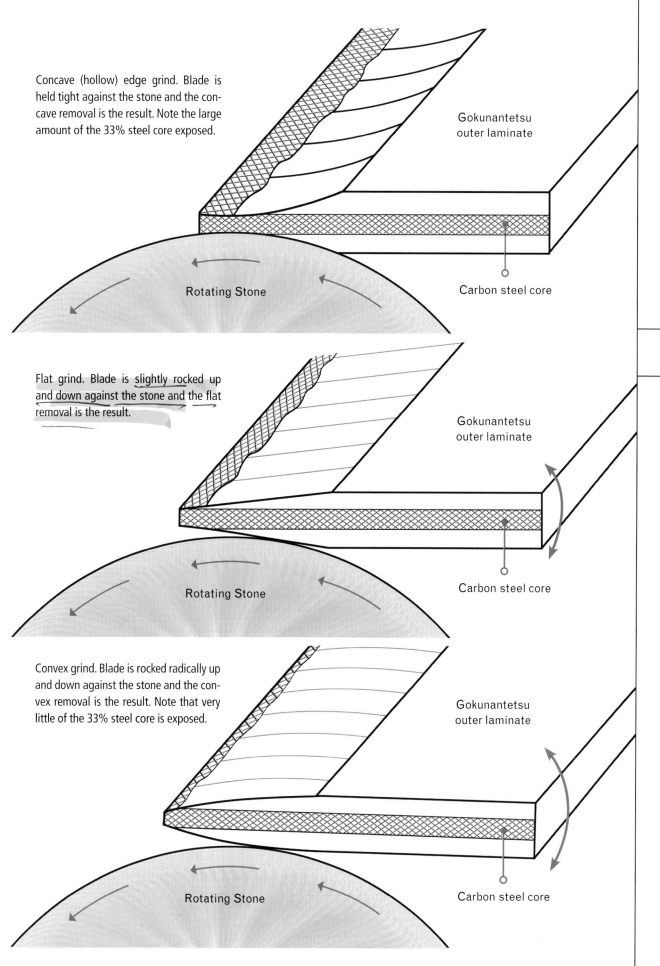

Concave (hollow) edge grind. Blade is held tight against the stone and the concave removal is the result. Note the large amount of the 33% steel core exposed.

Gokunantetsu outer laminate

Carbon steel core

Rotating Stone

Flat grind. Blade is slightly rocked up and down against the stone and the flat removal is the result.

Gokunantetsu outer laminate

Carbon steel core

Rotating Stone

Convex grind. Blade is rocked radically up and down against the stone and the convex removal is the result. Note that very little of the 33% steel core is exposed.

Gokunantetsu outer laminate

Carbon steel core

Rotating Stone

Philosophy of Japanese Metallurgy

There are many differences between Japanese bladesmithing and its western counterpart. Many of these differences are mechanical in nature and others are philosophical. Basically, Japanese blades are made with the function of cutting uppermost in mind. That may sound like obvious criteria, but you'll see that it is not the primary criteria for western cutlery.

First I'll explain the mechanical differences in the construction of blades.

Starting with the selection of raw materials, namely the steel, Japanese bladesmiths choose blade-specific steels, either those made by Hitachi "Yasuki Blue or White Steel" or special cutlery grade "Swedish Steel" (popular in the 60s and 70s). These steels have very high carbon content, usually not less than one percent and most between 1.2 percent and 1.4 percent. The carbon content determines how hard a blade will get, how sharp you can make it and how long it will hold an edge. These steels are tricky to forge, difficult to forge weld and are very unforgiving when heat-treating (annealing, quenching and tempering). Additionally, there is the extra step of forge welding this high carbon steel in an exacting way to mild steel.

Conversely, many western bladesmiths consider almost any steel 'useable' if it has carbon in it and if it will make a 'decent blade.' The carbon content hovers between 0.5 percent and 0.9 percent. Steel that is forgiving when heat treating is preferred to finicky steel. One senses that the steel chosen is more or less a means to an end and not overly important in itself. One rarely finds a bladesmith that is loyal to one steel and who has made hundreds of blades with dedication and passion to discovering all the secrets that lay hidden in the steel. (I can only think of one ABS Mastersmith who has dedicated his career to pushing the limits of 52100 ball bearing steel.)

Next to consider is the heat source to heat the steel to make it pliable to forge. The two most common sources of fuel for heating blades in North America are green coal forges and gas forges (LP gas, propane, etc.) Steel acts like a sponge when it is heated to, or past, the point of becoming red hot. Therefore, the atmosphere surrounding the heated steel is very important. An atmosphere full of polluting sulfur and phosphorus, such as in a green coal fire, will contaminate the steel, adversely affecting the hardenability and grain size of the finished blade. Likewise, a gas forge that is not regulated carefully will have an oxygen rich atmosphere, leading to the absorption of oxygen and giving up carbon in exchange. Less carbon results in less cutting performance in the finished blade.

Japanese bladesmiths, on the other hand, prefer to use coke (coal that has been heated in the absence of oxygen, to drive off the impurities) or pine wood charcoal as a fuel to heat their blades. Both of these fuels are very clean burning and provide a carbon-rich atmosphere for heating the steel.

Now let's examine the steps leading up to the most critical step in making a blade: quenching.

Most western blades are machined before quenching, i.e., the edge of the blade is ground to almost finished dimensions, thin at the edge and thick at the spine. This is to save time and material compared to trying to machine a fully hardened blade. To prevent this uneven blade from warping, twisting or cracking at the thin edge when quenching, the blade is annealed or normalized several times. Let's hope that the fuel source for these extra heating steps is clean and not oxygen rich!

Japanese blades are process annealed once and then are subjugated to a very severe process called cold forging. Rather than stress relieve the steel through a series of extra annealing and normalizing, the blades are actually stress induced. The Japanese blades are not machined before quenching, but

rather are hardened at full thickness to ensure an even hardness throughout the blade.

The quenching medium is a revealing indicator of the difference in philosophies as well. Western blades are usually quenched in oil, which is a slow and gentle quenchant. Japanese blades are always quenched in water, which is a very severe quenchant. If there are any hidden imperfections in the blade they will be revealed as it is removed from the violent water quench, as cracks and areas of delamination. It is a huge emotional investment to quench a blade in water after spending days forging and preparing.

Blade geometry is another area of difference. Western blades tend to be given a secondary edge bevel that will be strong enough to withstand the worst abuse imaginable for a particular kind of knife. This usually translates into a geometry that will not cut very well. Japanese blades are ground, after heat-treating, as thinly as possible for maximum cutting potential, with the understanding that the thin edge will have to be removed for those who are rough on their knives. If the knife edge chips, the steel is simply ground back to the depth of the largest chip, and the result is the perfect secondary blade geometry for the owner.

Final sharpening and honing is the *coup de grace* of differences. The primary edge of a western blade is commonly established with a rough mechanical grinder of some sort and then either stropped on leather or buffed on a buffing wheel. The result is an edge that is round in microscopic cross section. The Japanese blade receives a primary edge on the water-cooled rotating stone, and then it is meticulously hand honed on traditional water stones, first on a medium grit stone and then on a very fine stone. The result is an edge that is perfectly triangular in microscopic cross section. This kind of primary edge cuts very well.

We can clearly see that the careful selection of steel, the fuel for heating the steel, the degree of machining before and after heat-treating, the geometry of the secondary edge and the meticulous honing of the primary edge all give Japanese blades a distinct advantage in cutting performance. This is not to say that western blades are inferior, only that the philosophy is different. The focus of western bladesmithing is to create blades with outstanding toughness and durability.

The "Song of the Burr," a phenomenon only fully experienced and understood by graduates of Carter Cutlery Traditional Japanese Bladesmithing classes.

Simple, Rustic, Effective!

It is commonly said by Japanese bladesmiths that the customer pays for the blade of a knife and gets the handle for free. This of course is an exaggeration, but it does reveal a lot about how the Japanese smith feels about his greatest contribution to the customer, namely, a superior blade. To the smith, the 'superior' in the blade is metallurgical, and therefore not outwardly visible. The smith trusts that through use, the superior quality in the blade will be readily apparent to the owner.

Similarly, it is a common understanding that in order to continue enjoying the wonderful performance of the blade, periodic sharpening of the blade by the owner is necessary. Knowing that the customer will customize the geometry of the primary and secondary edges over time, the smith is not overly concerned with the exactness of the secondary edge symmetry. In fact, in the case of very high-end chef's knives, selling for thousands of dollars, the blade is often sold without a primary edge established. The understanding is that, for that kind of money, the chef buying the knife wants an edge of his choice and is willing to spend the time to grind it on. This helps explain why many Japanese blades seem to lack the symmetry and 'finish' of western blades.

Surface Finishing

Forged, polished finish next to forged, unpolished.

Six Surface Finishes Used at Carter Cutlery

A guiding policy for every Carter Cutlery blade is "ease of maintenance." All blades can be refinished in a matter of minutes at the shop and the cost to the customer is never more than a few dollars. The same cannot be said for expensive and time-consuming blade coatings. After much thought and experimentation, I use only six different blade surface finishes:

Forged, unpolished

Forged, polished

Hammer forged, unpolished

Hammer forged, polished

Ground, polished

Ground, polished, acid etched and buffed

The ***forged, unpolished*** finish is the simplest design in concept, yet it is by far the most difficult to execute properly, with no room for error. A blade is forged to within five percent of its final thickness, annealed, scale removed and then cold forged to its final thickness. It is heat treated and then straightened and secondary edge is ground. If at any time the flat of the blade is accidentally scratched, the finish is ruined, and must later be either polished or ground and polished according to the depth of the scratches.

The ***forged, polished*** finish is a nice combination of a blade that shines but still shows evidence of skillful forging and well placed hammer blows. It is accomplished by first cleaning the heat treated blade with the Japanese bocashi machine. This machine is little more than a large rotating brass wire brush that rotates in a trough of water. Fine mud powder can be added to the trough to effect faster cleaning. Following cleaning on the bocashi machine, the blade is polished on flap sanders. The flap sanders will polish the blade without removing the hammer blows or points of interest in the blade. Following the flap sanders, the blade can be polished on conventional muslin or stitched linen buffing wheels with buffing compound.

The **hammer forged, unpolished** finish is another finish that is difficult to execute perfectly. Following cold forging and prior to heat treating, the flats of the blade are hammered once again cold with a special hammer with a criss-cross pattern marred face. An irregular pattern is hammered on both sides of the blade. The blade is the heat treated and left as it is, making a stark contrast with the ground and polished secondary edge. Advantages of this finish include:

Hammer forged, unpolished finish Tactical neck knife (right) next to a forged, polished finish Long Original neck knife (left).

SURFACE FINISHING

Hammer forged, polished-finish tactical neck knife with mammoth ivory and ironwood handle.

The hand-held hammer with marred face responsible for the hammer forged finish on Carter Cutlery blades.

- Rustic look befits the image of a rural Japanese bladesmith product.
- Additional cold forging results in low and high areas of stress, possibly contributing to final cutting performance.
- Due to the irregular surface, this finish still looks great even after years of use.
- Possible advantage imparted for cutting materials with high water content, as indentations allow air to enter the cut negating the forces of capillary action.

The *hammer forged, polished* finish came about in the Carter Cutlery shop as a byproduct of an accidentally scratched hammer forged blade. The finished look is attractive and so now offered as a popular finish. As with the forged, polished blade, the blade is cleaned and then hit with the flap sanders and buffing wheels with compound.

Bottom Left: Blade being cleaned on the bocashi rotating brass wire brush machine.

Bottom Middle: Blade being polished on a 240 grit flap sanding wheel.

Bottom Right: Close up of flap sanding wheel in action. Keep in mind, the wheel is rotating up and away from the worker.

Before and after: Blade above is unpolished after heat treat, blade below has been cleaned on the bocashi machine, flap sanded and polished on the buffing wheel.

The **ground and polished** blade is the most common finish on factory and benchmade knives. Usually the flats of the blade are ground either by hand or with a surface grinder, and polished before the secondary edges are ground and polished. The result is a very shiny knife. The grinds of most kitchen knives, however, have a gentle convex edge geometry starting at the back of the spine all the way to the cutting edge. For this kind of grind and polish we use a 2X72-inch belt sander at very low speed. The belt rotates over the flat platen with a radiused PVC sponge insert attached to it.

The **ground, polished, etched and buffed** finish is uniquely used on Damascus (pattern welded steel) blades. After grinding both the flats and secondary edge and then polishing, the blade is immersed in a weak ferric chloride acid solution (sold as "Archer's Etchant" at Radio Shack). The amount of time the blade is left in the acid to etch depends on the steel in the Damascus, the strength of the acid and the desired effect. After the blade is cleaned and washed in a base cleaner to neutralize any remaining acid, it is buffed on the stitched linen buffing wheel with green compound. The advantage of this finish is that it is beautiful and can be redone in just the matter of a few minutes, keeping the cost of refinishing reasonable.

Above: From top to bottom. The stacked billet to be forge welded, the completed billet, the heat treated blade and the final buffed blade.

Right: Grinding a curved radius on a kitchen knife with the 2X72-inch grinder, the flat platen and a radiused piece of PVC sponge.

One common method in Japan for polishing blades involves the use of emery-coated stitched linen wheels. It is the most economical use of abrasives. A linen wheel of the correct diameter is coated in a special glue to which abrasive powder is attached. The glue is made from a variety of organic materials and must be heated to get it to the proper viscosity so that it can be coated with a brush along the outside diameter of the wheel. The freshly coated wheel is then rotated in a trough of the desired grit emery powder, left to dry and then attached to the mandrel of a motor. The abrasive is dressing for concentricity and then used to polish.

Sanding and polishing

Sanding and polishing the blade and or guard is usually done at the same time the handle is shaped, but in some circumstances sanding will be required before the handle is attached. Complex grind lines or flat secondary edges can be further accentuated by sanding by hand while the tang of the blade is held firmly in a bench vise.

At Carter Cutlery, polishing is accomplished using just four grits of sanding abrasive: #120, #220, #320 and #400. The lowest grit necessary to remove any deep scratches is used, followed by the next grit in a different direction. A finer grit is used in still a different direction, and so on, until the desired polish is achieved. It is im-

Valuable materials

Looking back at my earlier days of bladesmithing, I want to kick myself for not making the best use of the precious materials I consumed. I threw out 2X72-inch sanding belts after a few uses or when they clogged up with wood. I threw out small irregular chunks of steel. I discarded half completed knives. I threw out small pieces of ivory and ironwood, and other materials that were in my way. It is not that I didn't respect the materials I was using, I just simply didn't know any better, and my shop was piling up with half used up stuff that I didn't know what to do with, so I threw it out to keep down the clutter.

Now, I go to great lengths to make the very most out of every resource I have. I see every material as precious, and through experience have found ways to stretch everything I have. To me it is a matter of utmost respect for the materials and a satisfying efficiency in using every last gram of resource. To others it may look like I'm the cheapest bladesmith around, but in the end it just boils down to good economic sense.

For example, sanding belts give the longest service when used for wood first, then after a few hundred uses, they can be used for grinding soft metals such as brass, then they can be used for grinding steel. You can grind the outer profile of thirty or forty good size knives with a fairly worn out rough (#40) belt.

Now, it can get to the point of being silly, because time is money. Your time will always be worth more than a $4 sanding belt. Personally though, I get so much satisfaction from throwing out a completely used up grinding belt that I am often guilty of spending a bit more time at grinding on dull belts than the next guy does. But then again, personal satisfaction in knifemaking is very important to me. What good is it to be your own knifemaking boss if you can't do things your way?

Another way to make steel and handle material go the farthest is to design a few compact and miniature knives. Cut-offs too small for regular-sized knives can be assembled into smaller knives. It is amazing the number of fine knife customers who really appreciate a well made tiny knife.

A collection of "Carter's Clinkers." I never did find a good use for these naturally occurring beauties!

perative that, no matter what grit is finally used, the scratches from that grit all run in the same direction. A blade polished with #1000 grit sandpaper but with scratches running this way and that will not look as finished as a blade polished with #220 and the scratches all running in the same direction.

Sanding and polishing that follows rough grinding of the completed knife follows the same step procedure through the grits of sanding abrasives. Always finish all parts of the knife, i.e., the blade, handle and guard with the same grit before moving to the next. If you attempt to sand the handle with #220 grit but the blade has already been sanded to #400 grit, it is inevitable that some grains of #220 grit will find their way to scratch the blade.

Special attention should be given to rounding all corners on the knife handle. As you are sanding it, stop periodically to hold the knife in your hand. Make sure it feels comfortable. Here is your chance to make the handle more comfortable than most. Pay attention to handle-metal transitions,

Above: When finishing, pay special attention to wood/guard junction.

Above Inset: Scratches in a knife handle are revealed with buffing.

and sand down any edges that are sharp and uneven. When sanding the blade, pay attention to the straightness and evenness of the grind lines. When the whole knife is sanded to #400 grit, it is ready to be buffed.

The electric buffer consists of a linen wheel that is charged with buffing compound. We use two different buffing wheels at Carter Cutlery, one for metal and the other for handle materials. The buffer will really finish up a knife nicely if the whole piece was thoroughly sanded to #400 grit. If, however, there are some deep scratches hiding somewhere, the buffing process will reveal them. In this manner, the buffer is also used as a quality control measure. The buffed knife is examined closely in a strong source of light, and remaining scratches are removed by going through the hand sanding process again as necessary.

Polishing is achieved using: #120, #220, #320 and #400 grits of sanding abrasive.

A word of advice: When you do find a deep scratch that was revealed by the buffer, the temptation will be to try to remove any unsightly scratches with the finest sandpaper possible, i.e., #400 grit, thinking that this will save effort and time. Experience shows that it is much faster to drop a few grits to #220, remove the scratch, and then move up to #320 and finally #400. If, for example, it would take fifty strokes with #400 sandpaper to remove a scratch, the same could be done in less than twenty-five strokes by going #220, #320 to #400. Fifteen strokes with #220, five with #320 and five with #400.

Low Temperature Silver Soldering

Traditional Japanese bladesmithing employed the technique of silver soldering during the fabrication of some of the hardware attached to the Samurai swords. As these pieces were not soldered directly to the blade itself, it was not necessary to employ low temperature soldering. However, if the modern Japanese bladesmith wishes to create a kitchen knife with a metal bolster, or an outdoors knife with a metal guard, low temperature silver soldering techniques will be required. Solders that melt at around 210 degrees C are most commonly used.

To create a kitchen knife with a metal bolster or an outdoors knife with a metal guard, low temperature silver soldering techniques will be required.

To successfully solder a metal guard or bolster to a blade, follow these guidelines. The surfaces to be soldered should mate well, without unsightly gaps. The surfaces must be completely clean, and prepped by applying an appropriate acid flux. The pieces (blade and metal guard or bolster) are clamped together to eliminate movement and slowly heated with a torch. Additional flux is applied liberally with a proper flux brush. Care must be taken to not inhale any of the flux vapors as they evaporate from the heating workpiece. Evenly heat the area to be soldered and do not let an excessive amount of heat seep into the blade. When the metal and blade have reached the proper melting temperature for the silver solder, the solder will melt and flow into the void. The torch's flame is applied from the desired direction of solder travel. If you desire the solder to travel from top to bottom then the final heat is applied from the bottom.

Once an adequate amount of solder has been applied, the workpiece is allowed to cool to room temperature and any clamps are removed. The workpiece is thoroughly rinsed in clean running water to remove any traces of the acid flux. An acid neutralizer such as tri-sodium phosphate (TSP) can be used, but I do not find it necessary.

Top Left: Slowly heat area to be soldered, don't rush. Top Middle: Continually check with the solder wire for melting temperature. Top Right: Once solder starts to flow, ease up on the heat, only applying enough to keep the solder flowing until the whole area is completely soldered.

Right: Soldered joint is thoroughly cleaned in water and then washed with soap to neutralize any remaining acid flux.

Below: Silver solder can clearly be seen from the other side of the joint, indicating a perfect flow of solder through the joint.

Using daily carry neck knife to clean solder joint.

If there is concern about residual acid, the workpiece can be washed with some hand soap. The piece is then thoroughly dried

The blade is then clamped in a bench vise and the excess solder is removed from all surfaces. You can use any number of tools for this job, such as sandpaper, engraving tools or a piece of shaped brass, but I prefer to use my daily carry neck knife. Once the solder joints are cleaned up, they can be sanded lightly to finish the task.

Attaching Handles

A blade may have one of three types of tangs: a full tang, a hidden (rat tail) tang or a partial tang. Techniques to attach the handles will vary according to what type of tang the blade has.

The full tang knife

Full tang knives have either have a guard (bolster), or not. Attaching handles is different for each. Let's examine them separately.

A good knife needs a good handle.

Left: Six different handle options on the popular Carter Original neck knife. From right: Ebony, Celluloid, Bocote, Amber jigged bone, White bone and Macassar ebony.

Below: Full tang kitchen knives. From top: Nakiri, Wabocho, Funayuki and Western carving knife.

Different Types of Knife Tangs

Full Tang

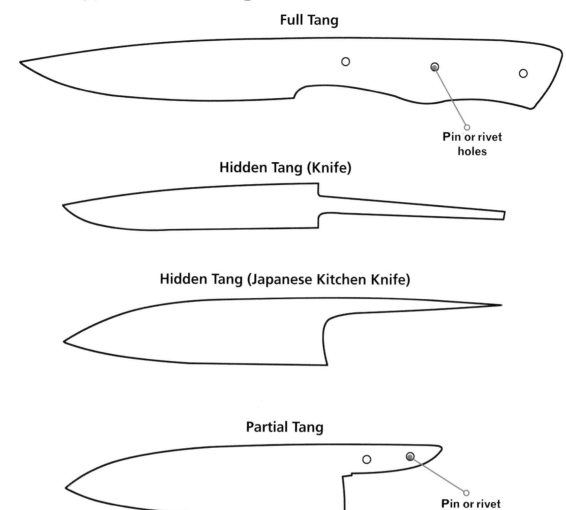

Pin or rivet holes

Hidden Tang (Knife)

Hidden Tang (Japanese Kitchen Knife)

Partial Tang

Pin or rivet holes

Two types of tang construction: full tang and hidden tang.

My biggest investment in handle material to date; a complete mammoth ivory tusk from Siberia costing $5600 at the time.

Above Top: International Pro Ultra Lite Series Funayuki in ironwood and copper/G-10 laminate bolster.

Above: International Pro Series No-Bolster Funayuki in ironwood.

Knives with a guard (or bolsters)

A suitable piece of handle material is chosen, either a natural material, usually an exotic wood, or a man-made material such as Micarta. In the case of a block of wood, the wood will need to be cut down the middle to make two halves. This can be done with the band saw or a hand saw. The outside is marked with a pencil to avoid confusion later. It is important that the grain of the wood lines up as it did before it was cut. The inside cuts are ground smooth and flat with one of the belt sanders.

The forward edge of one of the handle pieces is ground square and then held against the guard and viewed in the light. If there are any gaps in the guard/ handle joint, they will be visible when examined in the light. Grind the handle material carefully until it mates perfectly with the guard. If you have removed a lot of material in this process, it will be necessary to remove the same amount of material from the other handle piece before it is attached also. This ensures that the grain of wood will match when the knife is finished.

Clean the tang and guard with acetone to remove any oils or dirt, then mix some epoxy. The first side of handle material is carefully glued and clamped in place, making sure that the handle/guard joint is tight. Once the glue has set, the pin holes are drilled through the handle from the side of the tang. If the handle material does not follow the profile of the tang, now is the time to cut it close to the final dimensions.

Excess epoxy is cleaned off to allow attaching the other side of the handle. The forward end of the remaining handle piece is mated to the guard using the light to determine needed adjustments. Then the exposed

Above: Slabs of ironwood are cut from a block using the band saw.

Left: Book matched wood scales.

tang is cleaned again with acetone, new epoxy is mixed, and the remaining handle is glued to the knife.

After the glue has set, the pin holes are drilled using the existing drilled holes as pilot holes. The handle is now shaped using various grinders. Pin holes are left open until the handle is sanded to #120 grit. Then the pins

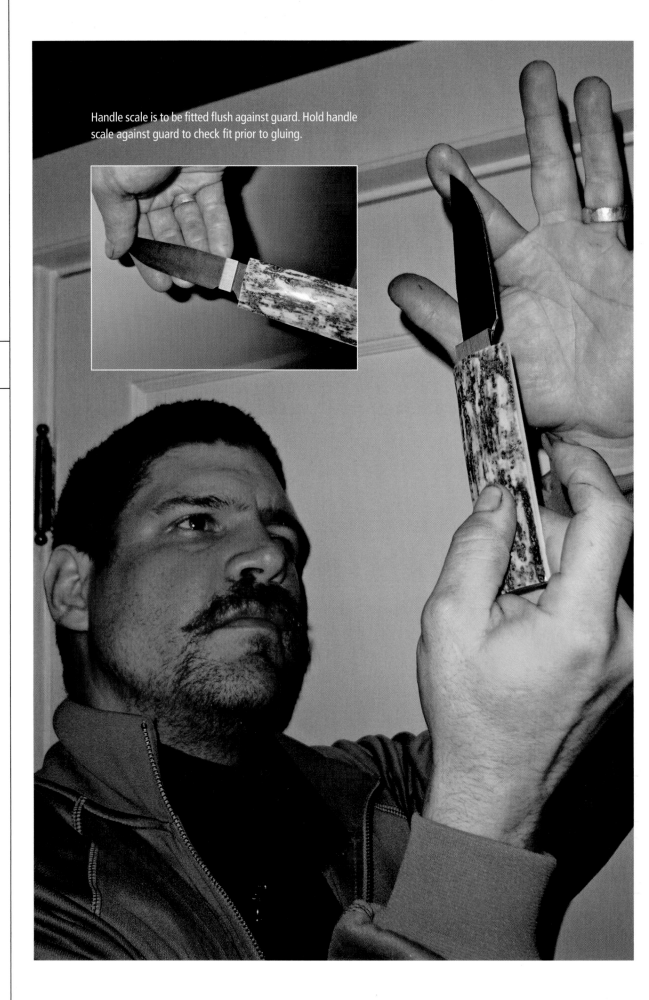

Handle scale is to be fitted flush against guard. Hold handle scale against guard to check fit prior to gluing.

are added, peened in place if necessary and ground flush with the handle. The knife is now fully functional, but requires sanding and polishing to look pretty.

Knives without a guard (or bolster)

The handle slabs for a guardless knife must be more carefully prepared than a knife with a guard. After the two halves of handle material are cut, mated and ground flat on the inside, pin holes are drilled in

PUT HANDLE INSIDES TOGETHER, TO MAKE SURE THEY ARE FLAT,

Below: Cut single side handle material from the full tang/guard knife.

The second handle scale has been carefully fitted and glued to the knife tang. Take care to match the natural grain of the handle material.

Top knife is only rough sanded to #120 grit but perfectly functional. Bottom Short and Stubby knife has been finished to #400 grit sandpaper then buffed.

Drill pin holes through the handle scale using the tang holes as pilot holes.

the handle material. This is accomplished by positioning one half of the handle on the tang and then drilling through the existing tang holes. As each successive hole is drilled, a tight fitting pin is inserted to keep the handle material from shifting as the next hole is being drilled. Before the pins are removed, the tang is traced onto the handle scale with a pencil, so it can be cut out with a band saw later.

The second half of the handle is closely mated to the first, the knife tang is flipped over, and holes are drilled through the second piece by using the existing holes in the first as a guide. Again, pins are inserted into each hole to keep the handle from shifting. The second handle scale is traced with a pencil, and then both pieces are cut close to the actual tang shape with the band saw.. Before the

CUT OUTSIDE OR THE TRACE

handle can be epoxied in place the final profile for the front of the handle has to be cut, tapered and polished.

If the blade is to be polished or buffed, it must be done at his time. The tang is cleaned with acetone and epoxy mixed. The handles are coated in epoxy, and attached to the tang with tapered pins made for this operation. The handles are clamped in place and excess glue at the front of the handle must be completely cleaned with acetone at this time. Any unsightly epoxy not completely removed will be a permanent feature of the knife, so spend the time to clean it well. Before the epoxy sets, the tapered pins must be removed. Twisting them as they are removed helps. The handle is the shaped using various grinders. The pin holes are left open until the handle is sanded to #120 grit. Then the pins are added, peened in place if necessary and ground flush with the handle. The knife is now fully functional, but requires sanding and polishing to look pretty.

How to remove stuck pins

If you should happen to forget a temporary pin in the handle after gluing the handle scales on, there is a simple solution, provided the pins are long enough to stick out from the handle scales. Light a gas torch and heat the pins in such a way that the flame is not directed at the knife handle. Let the heat in the pin transfer through it, thus breaking the bond of the epoxy. Carefully twist the pin using a pair of pliers. The pin will come right out. Be careful to not heat the pin so much that the heat burns the wood around the pin hole. If the pin is too short that you can't safely heat it, consider just leaving it in the knife, or risk drilling it out.

The tang is traced on the handle scale with a pencil.

Holes are drilled through the second handle scale by using the previously drilled holes as pilot holes.

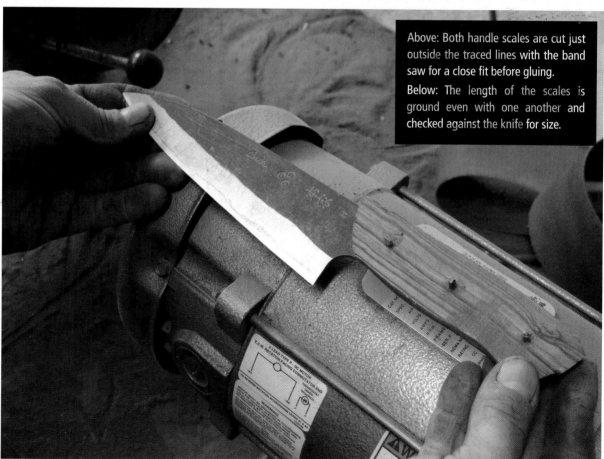

Above: Both handle scales are cut just outside the traced lines with the band saw for a close fit before gluing.

Below: The length of the scales is ground even with one another and checked against the knife for size.

The front of the handle scales are chamfered.

The chamfered scales are ground on progressively finer grit sandpaper, making minor adjustments along the way.

Top: The chamfers are checked for balance.
Bottom: Handle scales for full tang kitchen knife (no bolster), ground and polished before gluing.

The chamfered edges are polished on the wood buffer.

Peening a pin.

Close up of peening pin.

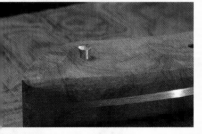

A solid pin is peened from both sides of the handle to make a mechanical fastener.

Pins, rivets and Loveless screws.

Pins, Rivets And Loveless Screws

In addition to adhesives, there are also several mechanical fasteners that can be used to help secure handle material to knives. The three most common fasteners are pins, rivets and Loveless screws.

Of the three, pins are the easiest to obtain, the cheapest, but also the most difficult to use. Pin material varies from brass to stainless steel and nickel (German) silver. A knife handle is drilled through the tang and the handle material for the appropriate size pin stock. When the handle has been ground down to within two percent of its final dimensions, pins are inserted and cut off with a couple of millimeters to spare on both sides. The end of one side of the pin is ground square and then "peened" with a hammer on an anvil to increase the pin diameter.

The pin is lightly tapped as far as it will go into the peened side of the handle material, and then the end sticking out the other side is ground down to within one millimeter of the handle material. It is then peened to increase diameter. Peening concludes when there is no more free play between the pin and the handle. Care must be taken not to over-peen as some brittle materials can crack if peened too heavily. Wood such as maple or rosewood is very forgiving when peening; ironwood and ivory are less forgiving. The exposed head of the peened pin is then carefully ground flush with the handle material.

Ready-made cutler's rivets are fairly straight-forward to use, but they are difficult to find and are generally good for only one type and size of handle. These rivets are commonly found on half tang kitchen knives. To use, one simply inserts the female rivet through the hole in the handle and blade tang, insets the male rivet from the other side and carefully hammers them flush with the surface of the handle.

Loveless rivets are a little tricky to use properly and also the most expensive to buy. They are a three piece affair: a screw shaft and two threaded wide washers. A special two step drill bit is used to drill the handle material to just the correct depth. The smaller hole is the size of the screw shaft and the larger hole is the exact size of the wide washer. These fasteners are usually inserted at the same time the handle is epoxied on, therefore the handle dimensions must be very close to the finished product before gluing. The exposed screw/washer combination is cut off with a hack-saw and then ground flush with the handle.

Inserting cutler's rivets.

Rivetted handle using cutler's rivets.

After the epoxy is well mixed, it is applied to both handle scales on the inside surface, and then the handle scales are touched together.

Wet epoxied handles are first touched at one end and then the other.

Handles are lined up and then touched together.

Left: Handles are then pulled straight apart.

Below: Epoxy glue should be evenly spread between both scales, and all parts of the inside surface should be coated with the glue.

Far Right: Assemble the handle and pins in place, then lightly clamp. Don't clamp so tight that all the epoxy is squeezed out of the joint!

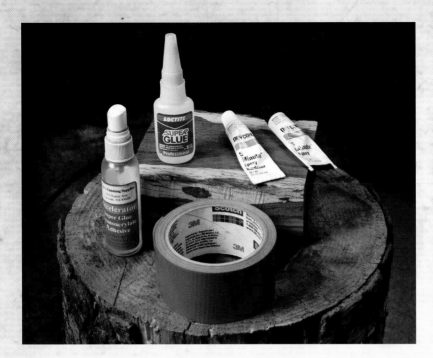

Left: Epoxy, super glue and duct tape.

Below: Shattered epoxy.

Accelerator in action.

Adhesives: Epoxy, Super Glue and Duct Tape

As a professional bladesmith forging and completing hundreds of blades a month, I find it necessary to keep a stock of various adhesives handy. Epoxy cement is a versatile adhesive that requires the user to mix two different liquids, part A and part B, for it to cure (harden). Epoxy is usually rated by the time it takes to begin to get hard, i.e., five-minute, 30-minute, one hour and twenty four hour epoxy. The rule of thumb is that the longer curing epoxies are stronger. Personally, I use five-minute epoxy for just about every gluing operation. I get excellent results provided I'm careful to use equal amounts of A and B and mix it extra thoroughly. I save a sample of epoxy from every batch I mix to test for hardness. Once it has cured for at least an hour I put it on my anvil and strike it with a hammer. Five-minute epoxy will shatter like glass if it has been mixed well.

Another adhesive that I couldn't be without is cyanoacrylate (Super Glue aka Krazy Glue). The most common use at Carter Cutlery is to fill voids and cracks in natural handle materials. The glue is applied to the voids, and then a special accelerator (hardener) is sprayed onto it.

It cures in minutes and can immediately be ground and polished. Another use for it is to apply a small drop to temporarily hold two pieces of material together for grinding or polishing. It's handy to have around to fix the kids' toys with too!

The knifemaking shop wouldn't be complete without a roll of duct tape. Among many uses, it's main function in our shop is as a base for mixing epoxy. A section of duct tape is taped to the surface of an anvil. Equal amounts of epoxy are mixed on it and used. The tape is then peeled away from the anvil and taped to the side of the garbage can. When the remaining glue on the duct tape is cured, it is tested with the hammer on the anvil.

Cyanoacrylate accelerator.

Super glue applied to small crack in handle.

Clean up the excess epoxy from the front of the chamfered scales, first with the epoxy mixing stick and then with a cloth and some acetone.

Cleaning with acetone.

Above: Before the epoxy completely cures, the temporary pins must be removed with a pair of pliers.

Once the epoxy has completely hardened, the handle is shaped and contoured on various abrasive mediums.

Hard to reach areas can be ground with small wheel attachments for the 2X72-inch belt grinders.

Pins are added and peened in place.

The exposed peened pin heads are ground flush with the handle.

The handle is then sanded by hand. The knife blade is clamped in a special vise called a "Knifemaker's Vise", which rotates the handle 360 degrees for final sanding.

The fruit of our labors!

Cord wrapped handles.

Full tang knives with cord wrap handles

Some full tang knives function well with a cord wrap handle. The knife that comes to mind is the very popular Kiridashi knife. The goal of the cord wrap is simplicity, ease of maintenance, slim profile and cost effectiveness. Therefore, complex wrapping techniques are not practical although they may look cool.

At Carter Cutlery, we employ the following simple technique for cord wrapping handles. If a slightly oval handle cross section is desired, cut

FIG. 1: First loop to start cord wrap handle.

FIG. 2: Hold it tight.

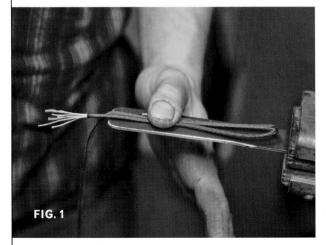

FIG. 1

FIG. 2

FIG. 3

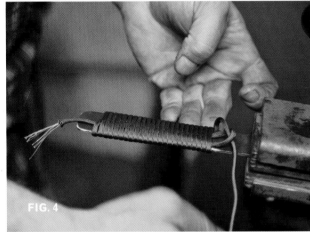

FIG. 4

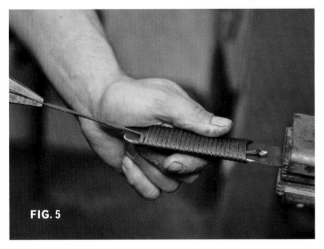

FIG. 5

FIG. 6

short sections of cord and glue them lengthwise along both sides of the tang. Cut a piece of cord eight feet long. Make a loop and place the loop towards the blade, with the short end of the loop slightly longer than the length of the tang. Start wrapping the long end from the end of the tang. When the wrapping reaches the exposed loop, thread the cord through the loop. Pull the exposed cord at the end of the tang to close the loop. Cut the remaining long cord off, leaving about three inches of cord. Continue pulling the exposed cord from the end of the tang until the loop and cut cord are pulled under the wrapped cord. Cut the exposed cord off and it is complete. The wrapped cord will not unravel.

FIG. 3: Cord wrap commencing.

FIG. 4: Cord end threaded through loop.

FIG. 5: Loop and cut end being pulled under wrapped handle.

FIG. 6: From start to finish: under five minutes.

Hidden tang carving knife with handle engraving.

High Grade Nakiri-bocho.

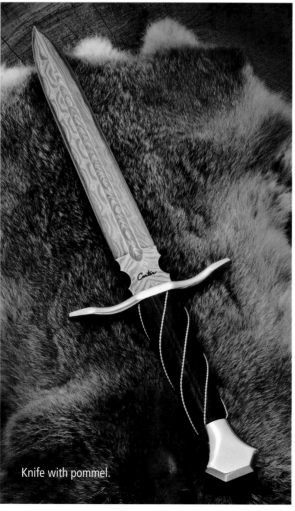

Knife with pommel.

Hidden tang knives

Hidden tang, or rat tail tang knives can have a guard (bolster), a pommel, or neither. I'll discuss each one.

Hidden tang knife with silver soldered bolster and pommel

A block of handle material is chosen for the handle. Until the bladesmith gains some experience it should be about twice as big as the desired finish handle, because of the difficulty in drilling the tang hole. It should be cut to length with about half an inch to spare. If the handle material is wood, the grain should run in the direction of the tang. The largest dimension of the tang is measured with a pair of calipers, and a drill bit about three quarters of that measurement is selected. The drill bit must be long enough to pass through the block of handle material. Hold the material in your hand with leather gloves.

Start to drill the hole in the center of the material, making sure that the material looks to be lined up straight with the drill bit. Every half inch or so, rotate the handle material 90 degrees one way, and then back again to check alignment, and keep drilling. It may be necessary to stop to clean debris from the drill bit. The drill bit will eventually emerge from near the middle of the bottom of the material.

The hole now has to be enlarged and made to match the dimensions of the tang. Some materials, such as ivory, bone, antler and synthetics, will require more drilling and filing to allow the handle material to fit on the tang.

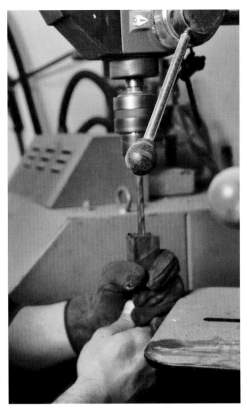

Left: Holding handle material and drilling hole for a hidden tang knife. Below: A hole drilled through the handle block.

Above: Various faux tang samples.

Many other materials and exotic woods respond well to burn fitting. It is done as follows:

Forge a bar of steel into the same dimensions as the knife tang, if an appropriate piece of scrap is not available. Heat this faux tang in the forge until it is red hot and then push it through the undersize hole. There will be smoke and flame, but the heat will cut the perfect shape hole. Check

Top: Orange hot faux tang will enlarge round hole to proper rectangular dimensions.

Middle: Burning tang in under-sized handle hole.

Right: A heated tang is used to enlarge a pre-drilled undersize handle hole.

the fit with the actual tang of the knife. The hole can be made larger if necessary by more burning or by filing.

Once the handle will slip on the tang, fit it to the bolster by holding up to the light and checking for gaps. Adjust as needed. Once a tight fit is achieved between the handle material and the bolster, the handle can be cleaned with acetone and epoxied to the tang. There are several ways to add the pommel, such as threading it on to the tang, pinning it with a pin or drilling it and holding it with screws.

Hidden tang knife with silver soldered bolster and no pommel

If there is no pommel in the design, then the hole for the tang must stop about an inch shy of the end of the handle. Otherwise, the steps are the same as for the hidden tang knife and pommel. Careful drilling and measuring is required to succeed with this design. Experience will be the best guide.

Hidden tang knife with no bolster and no pommel

Many of the traditional Japanese kitchen knives have a hidden tang, but no bolster or pommel. See Carter Cutlery's Kuro-Uchi Series, Stainless Fuku-Go Zai Series, High Grade Series, and Japanese Pro Series knives. In all cases, a wooden handle is prepared and an undersized hole drilled to within an inch of the end of the handle. The hole is made larger either with a faux tang forged specially for the purpose, or with the actual tang of the blade. The hole can be burned a little larger and then the tang glued in with epoxy, or the hole can be left about five percent undersize and then the tang hammered in by force. When hammering in by force, for a nice friction fit, care must be taken to not split the wood.

Attaching a Pommel to Hidden Tang Knife with a Threaded Screw

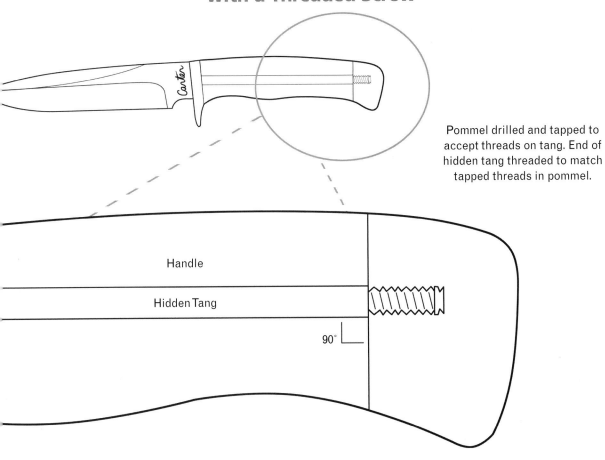

Pommel drilled and tapped to accept threads on tang. End of hidden tang threaded to match tapped threads in pommel.

Handle

Hidden Tang

90°

Attaching a Pommel to Hidden Tang Knife with Pins

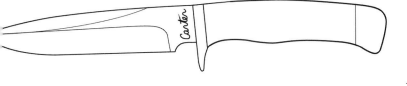

Small diameter metal pins are first epoxied in to tight fitting holes in the pommel. Drill slightly larger holes in the handle to allow for error. Fill holes in handle with epoxy and attach pommel. Maintain pressure until epoxy cures. (Hint: Use 5 minute epoxy).

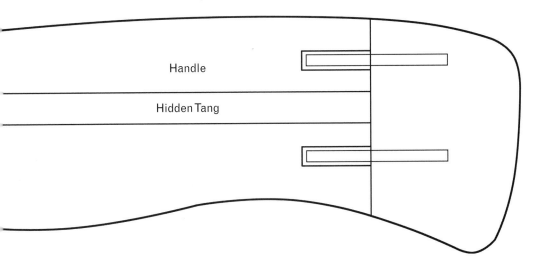

Handle

Hidden Tang

Attaching a Pommel to a Hidden Tang Knife with Screws

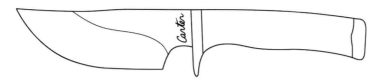

Two holes are drilled through the pommel, and one is drilled into the end of the handle. One screw is tightened in place, and the second hole in the pommel is used as a pilot hole through which to drill the second hole in the handle material. Fasten second screw.

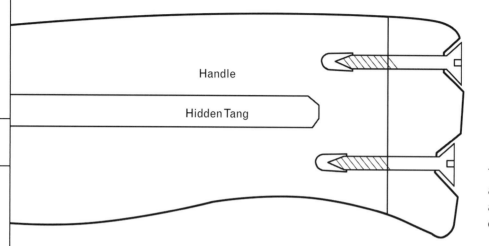

Handle

Hidden Tang

The handle is then shaped and sanded and finished according to the same procedure as a full tang knife.

Right Caption: Handle being hammered onto a hocho tang.

Partial tangs

Partial tang knives are not very common in hand forged blades because of the peculiarities involved in making handles for them. The only practical application for partial tang knives is for certain light weight kitchen cutlery, such as Carter Cutlery's line up of SFGZ-RH Series knives. High quality Japanese koshi-natas appear to have partial tangs, but actually they have regular length tangs and extended handles. It is easier in most cases to simply forge a full tang on a blade.

Sharpening

Before we delve into the sharpening instruction, it is imperative that you have mastered the "Three Finger Test of Sharpness." Here you'll discover the quickest and most accurate way to see if a blade is as sharp as possible.

There are many conventional methods of testing blade sharpness. One of the most common is to scrape the thumb of the left hand from right to left over the edge of an upward pointed blade. Another test is to see if a blade will shave hairs off of the forearm or slice newspaper. Herein lies a problem, as a dull knife with a burr can pass the first test, and a buffed knife (using a motorized buffing machine) can pass the second test of shaving. However, the buffed knife can usually be much sharper. Buffing the blade results in an edge that resembles the tip of a ball point pen microscopically. The edge is round, whereas a properly hand sharpened blade will have a completely triangular cross section.

Another thing that deserves mentioning is the controversial debate between what experts call a "smooth edge" vs. a "toothed edge." The usual conclusion to this

Testing the edge of a knife using the Three Finger Test of Sharpness.

Feeling the heel of the blade.

Feeling the belly of the blade.

Feeling the tip of the blade.

debate is that each type of edge will perform a certain cutting task better. I claim that the ideal "scary sharp" edge is one which is triangular in cross section, has microscopic teeth with give the blade "bite" and will also shave hair and slice newspaper with abandon. This kind of "scary sharpness" can easily be detected with the human fingers.

In the Three Finger Test of Sharpness technique, the blade's handle is held in the dominant hand, close to the body, with the tip of the blade pointed to the support side and the edge facing downwards. The thumb of the support hand is placed on the spine (or back) of the blade for safety and the first three fingers of the hand are pressed together side by side. This adds an element of safety, as pressure from the blade will be distributed over a larger surface area. Additionally, there are more nerve endings available to send messages to the brain. (Consider the sensitivity of the nerves of three fingers compared to the thumb.)

The three fingertips are brought into contact with the blade's edge and, ever so gently, you will attempt to slide the fingers not across but along the edge of the blade. The blade is tested this way along all parts of the edge, from the heel of the blade to the tip.

A totally dull edge will allow the fingertips to slide back and forth. No sense of danger will be perceived. A buffed blade that shaves will also allow the fingertips to slide, albeit the fingers will sense that the edge has a thin cross section and the brain will receive the message "don't push too hard." At a certain point of applied pressure, the round buffed edge would break the surface tension of the skin, resulting in a cut, but the brain will tell you to stop before that happens.

An edge accomplished in step five (grinding the primary edge) in our six-step sharpening procedure will give the fingertips the sensation of sharpness as little teeth in the blade's edge immediately want to "dig in" and therefore the blade won't slide along the three fingers. The brain tells you to not even attempt movement. However, the blade will probably not shave at this step.

Upon completing step six (edge honing), the fingertips will perceive yet a new level of sharpness, often referred to as "scary sharp." The little teeth in the edge of the blade are barely perceptible, and yet there is no sliding along the fingertips. The blade will also shave hair at this point.

Six-step sharpening procedure

Sharpening involves many steps, which led me to develop the "Six-step sharpening procedure." The steps are:

1. Rust removal, cleaning
2. Straightening
3. Profile adjustments
4. Blade thickness adjustments (secondary edge)
5. Grinding an edge (primary edge)
6. Honing

I will include the complete explanation of these six steps, but in most cases you can skip straight to steps five and six. The rest has already been covered in detail throughout this book.

Introduction

Cutting tools work more efficiently when they are as sharp as they can be. Most professionals who use cutting tools understand the importance of this statement. However, it is an unfortunate fact that at the domestic level, this simple statement of truth, which our great-grandparents took for granted, has been mostly forgotten. The blades we use at home for food preparation (kitchen knives) and for hobby (pocketknives, hunting knives) remain dangerously dull resulting in inefficient tools which often lead to frustration for the user.

The good news is that this situation can be remedied if the blade user is committed to acquiring the skills needed to keep their domestic blades sharp. The information presented here is intended not only to provide the technical information on how to sharpen "working knives," but more importantly, to provide some inspiration and motivation to do it, the elements which, when lacking, keep us from doing something that we think we would like to do. I trust that all audiences will benefit from my efforts, because it is these last two elements which I have really focused on, in this presentation.

How to sharpen a blade

When we understand that no blade is as sharp as a freshly sharpened blade, and that a blade used even once is duller then when it was freshly sharpened, we can assume that all blades which have been used will benefit from proper sharpening. Other methods that can be used to determine whether a blade needs sharpening are:

- The blade doesn't cut like it should or like it used to.
- It feels dull using the three-finger edge test.
- Light reflects off the edge when the edge is viewed under a good light source.

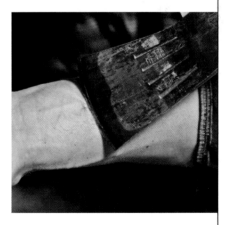

Top: Sharpening free-hand is quick, effective and rewarding.

Middle: Even an axe can be sharpened by hand in a short amount of time with outstanding results.

Bottom: How about an axe that is so sharp it can cleanly shave the fine hair on the inside of your wrist!

Clean the blade according to step one of six steps.

Check for straightness.

Blade with chips and broken tip.

TETSUO ☺

Once you have determined that a blade needs sharpening, the following procedure is recommended to obtain a sharp blade.

1. Rust removal and/or cleaning

With use or with neglect, blades and their handles can become dirty, soiled, stained, food ridden or rusty. The first step is to clean the whole tool to improve its overall condition and examine the blade better to accurately assess necessary steps.

Cleaning can be accomplished with hot water and soap on the handle and a soft abrasive cleanser on the blade. The blade is placed flat on a stable surface, cleanser is applied and rubbed back and forth with a rag until clean. Special attention is taken not to cut oneself during this operation. The cleanser will dull a blade, therefore, this step must be done before sharpening the edge of the blade (steps five and six).

2. Straightening

Check to see if the blade is straight. There is no such thing as a "perfectly straight" blade, however, any good quality blade, one worth sharpening that is, should look straight when examined by an educated eye. The proper way to examine a blade is to view the blade from the tip of the blade by holding the handle away from you. In this manner the whole of the blade is in view. If the blade's handle is held close with the blade pointing away, some parts of the blade are hidden from view.

The blade is first examined edge down, then edge up. Finally, the handle is held in the dominant hand, blade is pointed to the support side and he cutting edge is angled towards the viewer's eyes. This enables the examiner to see whether the blade is twisted, like a propeller. Bends and twists should be repaired or the blade replaced.

3. Blade profile and adjustments

Blades are occasionally abused or pushed beyond the limitations of their edge geometry (refer to step four) and the results are broken blade tips or chipped edges. These need to be assessed. If the damage is minor, i.e., less than 1-2mm (1/16 inch) or so, then usually it can be left the way it is to be eventually corrected by repeated sharpening sessions. If the damage is major however, it will most likely hamper the blade's performance unless corrected. Such a blade needs to be re-ground before continuing. Major repair is best done by a professional who has water-cooled grinding equipment.

4. Blade thickness, blade geometry (Secondary edge)

As a rule of thumb, all blades should be as thin as possible, have as acute an edge as possible, but be able to withstand repeated use.

With the exception of axes and bone chopping cleavers, most blades are too thick in cross-section and have edges which are too obtuse. This is why they don't cut well even with a shaving-sharp honed edge. Poorly designed blades, under the pretense of being built tough, are delivered to the consumer this way from the start. However, even properly made blades with appropriate thickness and good edge geometry will become too thick and the edge too obtuse after repeated primary edge grinding and honing alone. The edge progresses up into thicker metal as the thin metal is eventually ground away. If a blade has the proper thickness and edge geometry for the task at hand, the goal is to maintain these characteristics through proper sharpening methods.

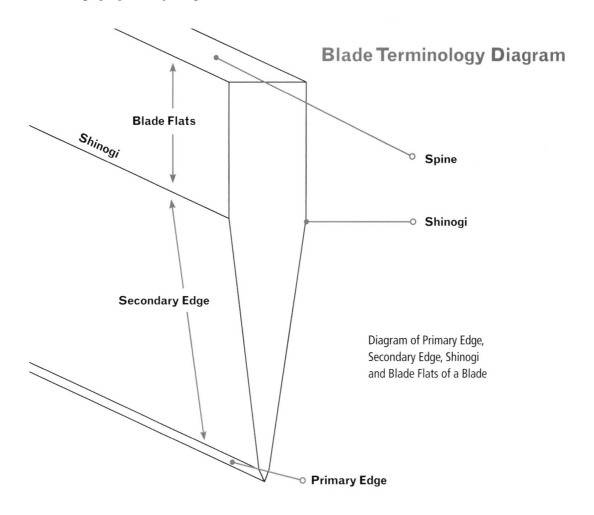

Blade Terminology Diagram

Blade Flats

Shinogi

Spine

Shinogi

Secondary Edge

Diagram of Primary Edge,
Secondary Edge, Shinogi
and Blade Flats of a Blade

Primary Edge

Machinist method
of determining blade geometry.
Start at the spine of the blade.

Slowly drag index finger
and thumb down to the blade flats.

Continuing in a slow steady
motion, drag them down to the shinogi.

There are two ways to determine if the blade is too thick or not. (Actually, you could just assume it to be so, and you would be correct 99 percent of the time.) The first method is to use the blade to cut something after the edge is sharpened and honed. Does it cut its intended material easily, or does it tend to "stick" in the cut? Does a kitchen knife slice easily to the bottom of the carrot or potato, or do they split while the blade is only half way ? General observation is the first method.

The second way to determine blade thickness is the "machinist's method."

This is done by holding the handle in the dominant hand while carefully pinching the back of the blade with the thumb and forefinger of the support hand. The thumb and forefinger are then gently slid down to the cutting edge slowly. After doing this repeatedly with several blades, the fingers accurately transmit messages to the brain of relative thickness and edge graduations. Blades considered to cut well and efficiently can be used as a gauge to compare to other blades. This is a highly accurate method of determining blade thickness and edge geometry once the skill is acquired.

If the blade needs to be thinned, this can be accomplished by laying the secondary edge, (the part of the blade directly behind the primary edge) flat on a coarse sharpening medium (i.e., #600 or #1000 grit water stone), moving the blade back and forth to remove metal from the thick areas. All areas of the blade are worked in a systematic order until the desired geometry is accomplished on both sides of the blade. Mentally dividing the length of both sides of the blade into overlapping sections, and then grinding each section in succession usually helps. Each section is ground five times back and forth and then visually examined before moving on to the next section. In this way, the blade is not likely to be over-sharpened, as only those sections needing more metal removal will be re-worked.

In general, metal will be removed the quickest in areas where the greatest pressure is applied. Thus, applying pressure towards the primary edge removes more metal just behind the primary edge, and pressure applied more towards the spine of the blade tends to improve the secondary edge geometry significantly by removing metal where it is the thickest.

The scratches in the blade due to the coarse grinding can be polished out later by repeating the same procedure as above, with a finer grinding medium (i.e., 2000-8000 grit water stone). Often this polishing step improves rust resistance and reduces cutting friction of the blade.

5. Grinding an edge, (Primary edge)

This is the phenomenon that most people associate with sharpening. While some specialized blades are sharpened down to an edge in the above step four (i.e.,

Your fingers finally end up moving over the secondary edge then the primary edge and finally off the blade completely and the thumb and index finger are left touching one another.

Secondary edge flat on sharpening stone.

Pressure applied to secondary edge near primary edge.

Pressure applied to secondary edge near shinogi.

Blade flat against the secondary edge.

Blade just barely high enough to clear the secondary edge, to establish primary edge.

Blade angle too high for fine cutting, but good for very heavy duty cutting chores.

the secondary edge and the primary edge are one and the same), most blades have a primary edge ground on them so that the blade will withstand repeated use.

Grinding the primary edge is accomplished by repeating the same procedures as in step four, with the difference being to raise the secondary edge of the blade off of the sharpening medium slightly.

Many authorities on sharpening offer suggestions as to what angle is best in terms of degrees (i.e., five or 10 gegrees) or an inclusive angle for both sides of the blade (i.e., 10 or 20 degrees). While not bad advice if used as a guideline only, there are two pitfalls to this way of thinking. First, most people who endeavor to sharpen blades have no adequate way to measure such angles while sharpening, let alone maintain such angles while the blade is in motion against the sharpening medium. Secondly, these angles do not take into account the huge influence of metallurgy, the requirements of different cutting tasks and the skill of the knife user. A blade of superior steel which has been heat treated properly can be sharpened at a lower angle for a given task than a blade of lesser quality. Also, a person who handles knives roughly will need a steeper edge on any given blade as compared to a very careful user.

Therefore, let experience be your guide. Raise the secondary edge from the sharpening medium just enough so that, as you grind a primary edge, you can just barely see a new bevel being formed when examined in the light. The advice "raise it just a hair" holds true here. Placing a coin on the sharpening medium and then placing the blade spine on the edge of the coin is one expedient reference that can also be used as a guide. For wide blades, or for a more "beefy" primary edge, two or three coins could be stacked together for reference. The coins are removed from the medium before the blade is set in motion.

The concept here is to have as thin as a primary edge as possible and then observe the edge occasionally in use to monitor it's performance. If the edge shows the signs of damage, such as miniature chips or curls at the edge, it can be immediately reground at a slightly steeper angle. (Which is why we always keep a sharpening medium handy when possible.)

The blade's primary edge is ground in sections on both sides until the bevels meet in the center along the whole length of the blade. The edge is then tested using the three finger technique.

Invariably, as you sharpen a blade free hand, without the use of stabilizing devices, there will be minor rocking of the wrist despite the best efforts to hold the blade at a constant angle to the sharpening medium. By keeping angles low to begin with, your achieved angle will be low or "just right" versus just right and "too high" (obtuse) an angle.

The object of learning to sharpen free hand is that you will not be dependant on a device for your results, enabling you to sharpen anywhere, anytime; and there is no artificial "skill eliminator" keeping you from directly experiencing the mechanics of sharpening, thus enabling you to acquire a skill and pursue mastery of sharpening.

6. Honing the primary edge

I also refer to this step as "stropping the edge." First the primary edge will be stropped with the coarse medium and then with the finer medium.

While the grinding procedures in steps four and five have been a back and forth motion (note: for steps four and five any grinding motion such as circular or left to right can be used so long as metal is being removed from where you intend), it is very important that all grinding in this last step be done with the primary edge moving away from the grinding medium rather than moving into it.

Although barely visible to the eye, the surface of the sharpening medium is covered in metal particles, particles of the medium and surface imperfections that you want your blade riding over rather than the edge bumping into, which would detract from your desired sharpening results.

Imagine trying to shave a postal stamp off of the sharpening medium. Now, move the blade in exactly the opposite manner, keeping the same angle as in step five. Start with the tip on one corner of the stone and move the blade backwards and sideways at the same time so that you end up with the heel of the blade at the opposite corner of the stone on the same side.

Five such stropping strokes are drawn on either side of the blade. Small metal particles that remain on the edge are called the burr. The burr is removed by drawing the edge, from the heel of the blade to the tip, through a soft piece of wood, twice, under the weight of the blade only. No pressure is applied. Then each side is stropped alternatively twice using less pressure. This procedure is then repeated using a finer sharpening medium (i.e., 2000-8000 grit stone).

This concludes the six-step sharpening process.

Remember to:

1. Use low angles.

2. Always strop backwards.

3. Monitor progress using the three finger method of testing sharpness.

Sharpening stone with arrow superimposed showing backwards direction of movement of stropping motion.

Above & Right: Blade being drawn through wood to nock off burr.

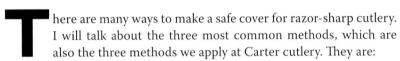

Making Sheaths

There are many ways to make a safe cover for razor-sharp cutlery. I will talk about the three most common methods, which are also the three methods we apply at Carter cutlery. They are:

- Leather sheathes
- Kydex sheathes
- Wooden scabbards

Bottom Left: Pouch-type leather sheath.
Bottom Right: Welt-type leather sheath.

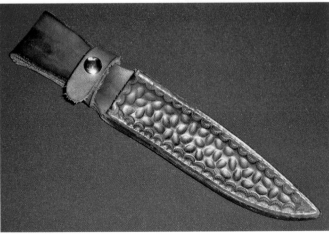

Leather sheathes

Leather is a truly amazing material that can be stretched, shrunk or formed to almost any shape imaginable. It is and always has been the choice material for covering blades. It is reasonably priced and can be worked with just a handful of simple tools. Modern leather comes in two forms: vegetable tanned (craft leather) and chrome tanned. Chrome tanned leather is not appropriate for knife sheaths, as salts remaining in the leather from the tanning process will cause blades to tarnish. Vegetable tanned leather, on the other hand, will not negatively affect steel if it has been tanned properly.

The two most common styles of leather sheathes for knives are the pouch-style sheath and the welt-style sheath. A pouch-style sheath consists of a piece of leather, roughly two and a half times the size of the knife, that is folded in half lengthwise and sewn together forming a pouch. A welt-style sheath consists of two pieces of leather, a front piece and a back piece, slightly wider than the shape of the blade, with a narrow strip of leather (the welt) separating them. These two pieces are sewn together with the stitches passing through the welt.

Kydex sheathes

Kydex is frequently used instead of leather in the knife industry. Technically speaking it is a thermoplastic, which means it is a plastic that can be formed into almost any shape after heating and will retain it's new shape after it cools to room temperature. Unlike leather which has a tendency to 'break in' after time and use, a kydex sheath does not lose its shape over time under normal temperatures. This makes kydex an excellent material when the issue of reliable retention is concerned. For knives which are to be carried upside-down in the sheath, or carried concealed next to the body, nothing is better than kydex as a sheath material. To use kydex:

1. Decide what kind of construction you will use (pouch-type sheath (one piece, folded) or pancake-style (two pieces).

2. Prepare a kydex press consisting of two pieces of one-inch plywood, 8x12-inches with one-inch PVC sponge glued to it with contact cement.

3. Open a bench vise just wide enough to accept the complete press when two halves are put together.

4. If using a pouch-type sheath, prepare by heating the kydex, folding it in half and letting cool. Drill the kydex and insert rivets in at least two places to prevent kydex from unfolding.

5. On a clean towel, heat the kydex with a heat gun slowly, keeping the nozzle of the heat gun at least eight inches away from the kydex. Keep the nozzle in constant motion to avoid overheating any one area.

6. When the kydex is pliable, quickly place the kydex on one half of the press, carefully (but quickly) insert knife into desired position, add the other half of the press and clamp in a vise.

7. After five minutes, unclamp vise and remove knife and sheath.

8. Add rivets to finish the sheath.

9. Cut and sand.

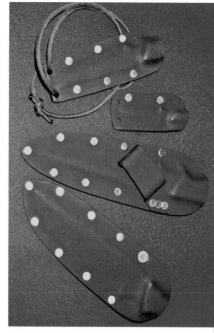

Variety of kydex sheathes.

Whitecrane knife with IWB kydex sheath.

Wooden scabbards

Wood is an excellent choice for covering the blade of a knife, and has been used as long as leather has. In its simplest form, a wooden scabbard is made by splitting an appropriately long piece of wood into two halves, hollowing out each side to the shape of the blade and gluing the two pieces back together again. The wood halves are often wrapped with cord or leather.

Another way to make a wooden scabbard is to split a length of wood into three pieces. The middle piece is shaped to the thickness of the blade and the blade outline is traced in the middle of the middle piece. The traced section is cut out of the middle piece and discarded. The three pieces are assembled and glued.

An example of a wooden scabbard on a Japanese Pro deba knife.

CHAPTER 16

What Dulls Knives:

How To Extend The Performance Of Your Blades

Knives go dull for reasons that most people would never think about. Knowing what causes blades to get dull, outside of legitimate use, will help you get more performance out of a blade between sharpenings. Let's examine the three most common types of blades: kitchen cutlery, pocket folding knives and hunting/camp knives.

The most common cause of blade dulling in the kitchen is knife abuse. By abuse I mean putting the knife in a dishwasher, storing the knife loose in a drawer with other cutlery and utensils, laying the knife on a cluttered counter top and dropping the knife into the kitchen sink when done using it. Other abuses include cutting food on a ceramic plate or marble countertop, and opening UPS packages with your fine kitchen blade (yes, I admit to having done this once or twice!) and prying frozen food out of its container with the tip of the blade. No doubt, abuse comes in other forms as well.

Even before you learn to properly sharpen blades, you can help keep your knives sharp by avoiding the above abuse of your blades. Just remember, anything hard can dull a blade.

Common causes for a folding knife to dull include many of the above, but usually the biggest culprit is overtaxing the design parameters of the knife. What I mean is that most folding knives are designed for light and precise cutting chores, not for heavy duty chopping and slashing, despite what many advertisers claim. Sure, you can use a folder for hard use (putting undue wear and tear on the knife that will ultimately shorten the usefulness of your knife) but you can clearly see that the blade will get dull the first time you use it for chopping and slashing. Same goes for digging in the dirt, scraping gasket material off of engine blocks and using the blade tip as a screwdriver.

Most of the above is obvious, but your folding blade can get dull as a result of getting dirty and dusty in your pocket. Wiping the dirt and dust off the blade results in some of the dirt and dust (which is often very hard) rubbing against the edge of the blade, thus wearing at the edge and contributing to its dullness. This is an incremental contributor. Keep it from getting dirty, or leave it dirty!

Carbon steel blades and carbon core laminated blades can get dull without use just by oxidation of the edge. Keeping the blades lightly oiled

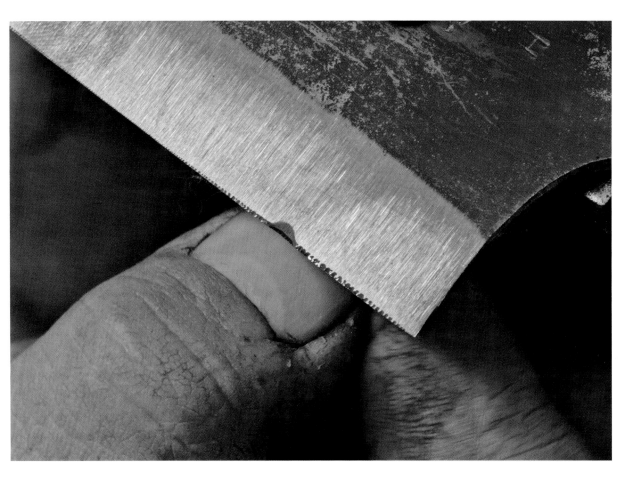

with either a modern chemical oil or non toxic natural oil is the answer. Some chemical oils preserve the blade longer (not better) but may prevent you from enjoying a slice of apple (or cheese, etc.) because your blade was covered in WD-40.

Hunting/camp knives can dull for all or some of the above reasons, but most hunting knives fall victim to something altogether different: neglect due to pre-conceived notions about the purpose of the knife. Hunting/camp knife owners often assume that the larger blade has more cutting power, and wrongfully conclude that the larger blades don't need the cautious care that smaller, thinner blades do. Remember, this topic is about how you can keep your blades from getting dull prematurely.

My ultimate goal is to encourage you to learn how to sharpen blades yourself (hey, you'll see that it's not as difficult as you think!), but keeping your blades as sharp as possible for as long as possible is a great skill to know.

Why some blades out-perform others

In preceding chapters you have read about the "Three Finger Test of Sharpness" and "The Six-Step Sharpening Procedure." Those essays help the blade aficionado understand what makes certain blades perform so well in their designed task, namely, cutting. By examining blade sharpening and practicing the six-step sharpening procedure, we can grasp the criteria that determine great blades through a process of reverse engineering. For example, when we encounter a blade that has a primary edge that is very thick and sharpened at a very obtuse angle, or when the secondary edge doesn't extend very far up the sides of a knife that is made from very thick bar stock, we can surmise that it won't cut very keenly.

Perfectly heat-treated Hitachi steel at a Rockwell hardness of 64 RC should flex and then return true.

The cutlery industry seems to follow the notion that a knife has to be thick enough and strong enough to withstand the worse abuse, at a sacrifice of cutting performance. My philosophy is that a blade should be designed for cutting. My rule of thumb is that all blades should be as thin as possible, but still hold up to repeated normal use.

By now you will have gathered that the geometry of the blade is very important to cutting performance. The other criteria for high performance cutlery, in order of importance, are as follows:

1. Blade geometry
2. Ease of maintenance
3. Durability
4. Edge sharpness
5. Edge holding ability

The ease at which a blade can be maintained at top performance is vitally important and thus is second on our list, ahead of sharpness and edge retention, which may come as a surprise to some. Namely, we want to be able to re-sharpen a blade easily. If two different blades were equal in edge retention, and the same technique for sharpening was used, the blade that sharpened the quickest is better.

Is that blade an asset or a liability?

All of us buy and acquire things for various reasons. Sometimes we genuinely need something for our day to day activities, such as a toothbrush to brush our teeth, and other times we purchase items simply because we desire to have them. I think that either motivation to purchase is legitimate if the buyer stops to consider the Asset/Liability concept. Considering the following questions will help you determine the value of each knife you have:

Is this for day to day use?

Is this for an investment?

If you spend X amount of money on a knife purchase, and you use the knife several times a week, or even daily, then the cost-per-use of that knife is less and less the more you use it. For example, if you buy a $100 knife, and use it 100 times per year, for ten years, then your cost is 10 cents each time you use it. On the other hand, if you use that same knife just a couple of times during ownership, it could cost you upwards of $50 per use.

Keep in mind that a knife that is used even once is no longer in mint condition, thus subtracting greatly from it's value on the second-hand market. This brings us to the second question, is the knife purchased for an investment?

Some knives, especially those made by prolific and highly sought-after custom knife makers, can be sold on the second-hand market for more than the knives were bought for. Usually the price difference corresponds to the passage of time. Wouldn't it be great to receive 20 percent interest on a knife investment over a couple of years! Let's say that your $100 knife, never used, is sold for $120. You made $20 profit...or did you? You see, every time you moved that knife around your home from one storage spot to the next, every time you took it out and cleaned it, it cost you time and effort. Surely your time and effort are worth something in terms of dollars and cents. I'd argue that your profit in this case was much less than the $20 you thought you made.

So where does that leave us?

Is your knife working for you, or are you working for it?

Knives that are constantly being used pay for themselves and are an asset to you. Knives that are carefully chosen for investment purposes might prove to be an asset over time. But the knife that is bought on impulse and then rarely used, it is clearly a liability to you...unless you are able to positively answer the following question in the affirmative:

Do I just have to have it regardless of the cost to me?

If you answered yes to that question, that's okay too, as long as you realize you are paying to pursue your hobby. By the way, having a hobby is one of the greatest expressions of freedom. And freedom is never free!

Durability means that the knife, both handle and blade, must not fail or break during normal use.

Note that, while not listed in the criteria above, it is assumed that ergonomics of a knife are the most important consideration of high performance cutlery. Good ergonomics are achieved when the handle and blade are designed to effectively and efficiently transfer the power and control of the users hand to the edge of the blade.

How to store cutlery long term

Even in the best of times, sometimes a person can't avoid the necessity of storing his personal belongings for a prolonged period of time. Perhaps he is off to study away from home, sent away on an out of town work assignment or simply is between permanent living accommodations. Whatever the cause, cardboard boxes are procured and the belongings packed away in them. Some of the packed things will likely remain in the exact same condition months or years later (books, pottery) and some might not (wool clothes, devices including batteries, etc.).

This brings us to the question of the owner of more knives than he can take with him: What is going to happen to my knives if I store them, and what can I do to protect them?

There is both good news and bad news for the person asking this question.

The good news is that, short of a natural disaster or high moisture, the knives will still be there when the boxes are reopened, more or less in the same shape as when they were packed away. Knives are fairly permanent things, and it takes a lot to make a knife perish.

The bad news is that, thanks to the second law of thermodynamics, commonly known as entropy, all materials on earth are constantly breaking down into their most basic elements. As complicated as that sounds, it simply means that steel will rust, brass and nickel silver will tarnish, and handle materials will age. How much aging will happen while the knives are packed away is anybody's guess, but one thing is certain, it will be more than if the knives were being looked at and tended to every couple of weeks or so.

So, in conclusion, try to avoid packing your knife collection in storage if you can. Maybe you have a dear trusted friend or family member who likes knives as much as you and who would be willing to baby-sit them while you are gone. Have them give them a once-over every month or so until you come back. Ideally, the knives would remain in better condition than packing them away.

If that solution isn't feasible, here are some suggestions on how to pack your knives away and still feel like you can sleep soundly at night:

1. Always remove knives from leather sheathes.

2. Treat leather sheathes with a leather preserving product and store in a separate box from knives.

3. Clean the blades of knives with acetone, being careful to not get acetone on any non-metal part of the knife.

10.5 sun Shiki-bocho in blue Corian™ handle and saya (sheath), black Micarta®, stabilized blue maple, white Corian and a red liner.

4. Oil or wax the blades with favorite product, applying product with a clean towel or tissue and NOT with fingers.

5. Wrap the blades in a clean piece of glossy color newsprint (not black ink pages).

6. Tape newsprint in place, but not directly to the steel.

7. Holding the wrapped blade, wipe the rest of the knife with preferred oil or wax product, taking special care to reach all the nooks and crannies. Use a cotton swab in the tight places if necessary.

8. Wrap the whole knife in something soft of your choice; clean towel, newsprint, bubble wrap, etc.

9. Place carefully into a box and mark the box on all sides indicating there are knives in it.

10. Choose the location for storage wisely; avoid areas like the garage (moisture) or attic (wide temperature variations).

11. Try not to lose any sleep while you are gone.

There you have it. I hope you found this advice useful. Feel free to pass this on to your friends.

How to sharpen anywhere, with anything

I explained earlier how to achieve razor sharp cutlery using simple sharpening stones. The technique I use is proven and very effective. What, though, are we to do if we do not have our stones handy and need to sharpen a knife?

The first thing you need to do when you find yourself in this situation of peril is sit down, relax and don't panic! Just kidding. All you have to do is look around for something that is harder than tempered steel. How about the rocks under your feet, or the curb in the driveway, or a cement foundation? Some other things to consider are the back sides of pottery and ceramics, sand paper, the diamond file on your Leatherman Tool or a carbide bit from another cutting tool.

I once refurbished the edge on my neck knife using an old 2x4 board that had been trampled into the ground for years. The dirt that was imbedded into the wood made a great abrasive. The long flat surface made it easy to make long sharpening strokes and sped up the job to under a minute.

Once you have found your sharpening system, the trick is to only sharpen by using the stropping technique. It is very important that all grinding in this technique be done with the edge moving away from the grinding medium rather than moving into it.

Imagine trying to shave a postal stamp off of the sharpening medium. Now, move the blade in exactly the opposite manner. If the sharpener is too small to move the blade against it, it will be necessary to immobilize the blade and move the sharpener.

Strop both sides of the blade. Small metal particles that remain on the edge are called the burr. The burr is removed by drawing the edge, from the heel of the blade to the tip, through a soft piece of wood, twice, under the weight of the blade only. No pressure is applied. Then each side is stropped alternatively twice using less pressure.

If you are satisfied with the new edge according to the three finger test of blade sharpness, you can try further refinement using a piece of cardboard or newspaper. Several backward passes on the paper should give you a hair-shaving sharp edge.

So, for fun or for profit, try this emergency sharpening secret and you will be well on your way towards mastering the art of free-hand blade sharpening.

Dilemma: Depend on one knife, or keep a spare?

There are some knife authorities who advocate that knife aficionados keep a spare knife on their person, in razor sharp condition, and to never use it unless a matter of life and death comes before them. The rationale here is that the pristine razor sharp edge will save the day. I strongly disagree.

There is much argument against the above advice. First and foremost, if you are presented with a life or death situation and your last resort is your knife (Heaven forbid it! You can still own a handgun in this country, you know!) then you need a familiar knife. You need one that feels comfortable and natural in your hand if you are to use it effectively and unconsciously. You will need the knife that you use most often, and know how to reflexively draw and present into action. By comparison, your body won't have developed the 'muscle memory' needed to access the unused, razor sharp knife. Muscle memory is the only way you'll get a knife in your hand when in the stress of a "flight or flight" situation.

On a whim, I check to see if the edges on my knives are up to the task of shaving.

By using Ol' Reliable you'll know what to expect when the blade meets some resistance, and it will be less likely to be jarred from your hand as would an unfamiliar knife. Incidentally, while it is true that a really sharp knife cuts easier, a knife doesn't have to be razor sharp to cut or stab when brute force is applied. (Think about all the nasty accidents that occur with dull knives.)

Another point to consider is that the so-called razor sharp knife may not be razor sharp after all. I mean, whose opinion are you going to trust on that one? Unless you actually cut things with it, how are you going to know if it is really sharp or not? Now, if you go through with that process of examination, may I suggest that you now have enough experience and knowledge to start keeping Ol' Reliable sharp yourself, via sharpening on a regular basis!

My recommendation is to rely on one knife and to use it as often as you can. Get to know what it can do, and what it cannot do. Learn how to maintain it and sharpen it. Let it become a part of you and one day it just may very well save the day.

CHAPTER 17

What Makes a Knife Special?

Humans throughout all ages and cultures have converted inanimate things into animate objects of desire. The Japanese have their three national kokuhou treasures: the sword kusanagi, the mirror Yata no kagami and the jewel Yasakani no magatama. In fact, it is a custom to give samurai swords personal names. Other countries have their crown jewels and items of great value and cultural identity. Here in the United States we have the Liberty Bell, the Statue of Liberty and our precious cars, to name but a few. Despite being composed of common materials such as wood, metal and glass, these objects have taken on a life of their own in our eyes. Indeed, battles to the death have been fought over objects, as if it were our own flesh and blood we were fighting for. What is it that makes objects seemingly come to life?

In the world of knives the same phenomena exists. Out of a large (or small) collection of knives, invariably one knife will stand out to us as the irreplaceable one. Perhaps it was Grandpa's pocket knife, its blades lovingly

An Alaskan skinner in bright orange G-10 handle scales.

Various neck knives ready for everyday cutting chores.

ground down to half their original size. Or perhaps it is the folder that has been faithfully carried in the right front pocket of our jeans for the past several years. For a combination of reasons, we have become firmly attached to this knife and would be dealt a devastating blow if it were lost or stolen. The very definite purpose of a knife may explain some factors that contribute to the formation of this emotional attachment.

First on the list is the performance of the blade itself. A knife is designed to cut, and the more the knife is used the more apparent the advantages will be of one knife over another. There really is something special about a razor-sharp knife that, once experienced, will be hard to live without. Superior cutting performance also factors in blade shape and geometry and ease of sharpening. If other factors also come into play, a superior cutter can likely be held on to dearly and perhaps become that special darling with a personal name. The saying "pretty is as pretty does" comes to mind.

Scribing patterns on forged billets of steel, my teacher's hammer is in the foreground.

My personal neck knife.

I'm accompanied by my first administrative assistant, Tim McCalla, upon Tim completing his first neck knife.

Feel in the hand contributes greatly to a favorite knife being chosen. Of all the hand-held tools and instruments, nothing is more fundamental than a knife. Not only must the handle be soft and inviting to hold, but, to be effective, it has to be firm and stout enough to expertly transfer the power and control of the hand to the cutting edge of the blade. The very finest knife handle will have been shaped and sanded by the human hand. This is an area where the custom bladesmith can excel.

The materials used in the knife's construction will greatly influence its perceived value. Natural materials generally have more appeal than synthetics. Even without considering any other merits or demerits, it is hard to ignore a knife handled in a fine mother-of-pearl or ivory handle. Besides these two premium materials, there is an assortment of others consisting of jigged bone, stag antler, buffalo horn and various exotic hardwoods, with ironwood standing out as a recognized favorite. A pretty knife will generate pride in ownership.

The size of the knife also greatly affects its appeal. Generally speaking, the knife we choose to carry and use everyday is the one that is going to grow on us the most. There is great value in a knife that proves itself useful. For this reason, almost all special knives, in North America at least, are smaller knives, either short fixed blades or folding knives.

Association can be another important factor. If the knife was a personal belonging of a loved one, either living or passed away, the knife can inspire a very personal attachment. Perhaps the knife didn't have a previous owner, but was a gift from someone special. In the case of association, often severe shortcomings in the overall design such as poor handle, blade shape or cutting performance will be joyfully overlooked.

Glossary of Japanese Terms

Akatsuchidoro – a special red mud clay primarily used in Japan for construction, but used in the traditional Japanese bladesmith shop for thinly coating blades before quenching.

Baikin – the Japanese word for germs.

Gokunantetsu – mild steel used primarily as a toughening outer laminate on Japanese laminated blades.

Hineribo – a bar or stick with a slot cut into it to torque twisted blades straight.

Kata-ha – literally "one edge," a two-layer laminate usually consisting of a hard carbon steel layer and a soft gokunantetsu layer.

Kobuse – a style of blade construction, primarily found in modern samurai sword blades, consisting of a mild steel core with a hard carbon steel wrap around the outside.

Kumamoto – a prefecture in southern Japan where Murray lived for 18 years.

Magebo – a bar or stick with slots cut into it to straighten a bent blade.

San-mai – literally "three layers," usually referring to a blade with soft gukunantetsu or soft stainless cladding to a hard carbon steel core.

Shinogi – the ridge line separating the secondary edge on a blade from the blade flats.

Tagane – a hammer with very hard carbide bits used to straighten bent or twisted blades by displacing small amounts of steel. Also a tool used for dressing Japanese rotating water stones.

Tsukareta – literally "tired," a word used to describe a Japanese sword that has been sharpened over the years to the point where it is no longer serviceable because the hardened steel is all removed.

Bibliography

The following books are suggested for further study:

Andrews, Jack. *Edge of the Anvil*. Emmaus, PA: Rodale Press, 1977

ASM International. *Heat Treater's Guide*. Materials Park, OH: ASM International, 1995

Bealer, Alex. *The Art of Blacksmithing*. Edison, NJ: Castle Books, 1969

Bottomley, Ian. *Arms and Armour of the Samurai*. Greenwich, CT: Brompton Books Corp, 1988

Boye, David. *Step by Step Knifemaking*. Emmaus, PA: Rodale Press, 1977

Brandt, Daniel A. *Metallurgy Fundamentals*. S. Holland, Il: The Goodheart-Willcox Co., Inc. 1992

Coe, Michael D. *Swords and Hilt Weapons*. London, England: Multimedia Books Ltd., 1989

Figiel, Leo S. M.D. *On Damascus Steel*. New York, NY: The Print Center, 1991

Hitachi Kinzoku Kabushiki Gaisha. *Isotropy*. Tokyo, Japan: Hitachi Kinzoku Honsha, 1995

Hrisoulas, Jim. *The Complete Bladesmith*. Boulder, CO: Paladin Press, 1987

Hrisoulas, Jim. *The Master Bladesmith*. Boulder, CO: Paladin Press, 1991

Kapp, Leon/Hiroko. *The Craft of the Japanese Sword*. Tokyo, Japan: Kodansha, 1987

Lee, Leonard. *The Complete Guide To Sharpening*. Newtown, CT: Taunton Press, 1995

McCreight, Tim. *Custom Knifemaking*. Harrisburg, PA: Stackpole Books, 1985

Nihon Kikaku Kyokai. *Metals Data Book*. Tokyo, Japan: Japanese Standards Association, 1992

Sachse, Manfred. *Damascus Steel*. Dusseldorf, Germany: Verlag Stahleisen, 1993

Satou, Kanzan. *The Japanese Sword*. Tokyo, Japan: Kodansa International, 1983

Shibata Shoten. *Houchou to Toishi (Knives and Sharpening Stones)*. Tokyo, Japan: Shibata Books, 1999

Smith, Cyril Stanley. *A History of Metallography*. Chicago, IL:University of Chicago Press, 1960

Zemansky, Mark. *Temperatures Very Low and Very High*. New York, NY: Dover Publications, 1964

Where to Get Supplies

Centaur Forge
117 N Spring St., Burlington
WI 53105
Phone: 262-763-8350
www.centaurforge.com

Ironwood by Don, AZ
14301 Aveneda Red Roan
Sahuarita AZ 85629

Jantz Supply
309 W Main
Davis, OK 73030

Knife & Gun Finishing
Supplies
1972 Forest Ave
Lakeside AZ 85929

"L. Brand" Coke
Ed Avolio
Phone: 800-441-0616

Sheffield Knifemakers
Supply
P.O. Box 741107
Orange City, FL. 32774

Texas Knifemaker's
Supply
10649 Haddington # 180
Houston, Texas 77043

Tru-Grit Inc.
760 E. Francis Unit N
Ontario, CA 91761

WHERE KNIFE COLLECTORS CONNECT WITH KNIFEMAKERS

The Knife Showcase at **BladeMag.com** is the premier site for knife-collecting. Chat with knifemakers, visit their blogs, find other collectors, or buy knives. Whatever it is that you love about knife-collecting, you'll find it in the Knife Showcase.

JOIN US TODAY.
click on Knife Showcase at www.BladeMag.com